ON THE NATURE OF THE PSYCHE

from
The Collected Works of C. G. Jung

VOLUME 8

BOLLINGEN SERIES XX

Also available in Princeton/Bollingen Paperbacks:

THE PSYCHOLOGY OF THE TRANSFERENCE by C. G. Jung, translated by R.F.C. Hull, Extracted from *The Practice of Psychotherapy*, Vol. 16, Collected Works (P/B Paperback #158)

PSYCHOLOGY AND EDUCATION by C. G. Jung, translated by R.F.C. Hull, Extracted from *The Development of Personality*, Vol. 17, Collected Works (P/B Paperback #159)

ESSAYS ON A SCIENCE OF MYTHOLOGY by C. G. Jung and C. Kerényi, translated by R.F.C. Hull (P/B Paperback #180)

THE ORIGINS AND HISTORY OF CONSCIOUSNESS by Erich Neumann, translated by R.F.C. Hull (P/B Paperback #204)

FOUR ARCHETYPES: MOTHER/REBIRTH/SPIRIT/TRICKSTER by C. G. Jung, translated by R.F.C. Hull, Extracted from *The Archetypes and the Collective Unconscious*, Vol. 9, part I, Collected Works (P/B Paperback #215)

AMOR AND PSYCHE: THE PSYCHIC DEVELOPMENT OF THE FEMININE by Erich Neumann, translated by Ralph Manheim (P/B Paperback #239)

ART AND THE CREATIVE UNCONSCIOUS by Erich Neumann, translated by R.F.C. Hull (P/B Paperback #240)

COMPLEX/ARCHETYPE/SYMBOL IN THE PSYCHOLOGY OF C. G. JUNG by Jolande Jacobi, translated by Ralph Manheim (P/B Paperback #241)

THE SPIRIT IN MAN, ART, AND LITERATURE by C. G. Jung, translated by R.F.C Hull, Vol. 15, Collected Works (P/B Paperback #252)

MANDALA SYMBOLISM by C. G. Jung, translated by R.F.C. Hull, Extracted from *The Archetypes and the Collective Unconscious*, Vol. 9, part I, Collected Works (P/B Paperback #266)

TWO ESSAYS ON ANALYTICAL PSYCHOLOGY by C. G. Jung, translated by R.F.C. Hull, Vol. 7, Collected Works (P/B Paperback #268)

ON THE NATURE

OF

THE PSYCHE

C. G. JUNG

TRANSLATED BY R. F. C. HULL

BOLLINGEN SERIES

PRINCETON UNIVERSITY PRESS

PUBLISHED BY PRINCETON UNIVERSITY PRESS, PRINCETON, N. J.

Extracted from *The Structure and Dynamics of the Psyche,* Vol. 8 of the *Collected Works of C. G. Jung.* All the volumes comprising the *Collected Works* constitute number XX in Bollingen Series, under the editorship of Herbert Read, Michael Fordham, and Gerhard Adler; executive editor, William McGuire.

FIRST PRINCETON / BOLLINGEN PAPERBACK PRINTING, 1969

Third Printing, 1973

LIBRARY OF CONGRESS CATALOG CARD NUMBER: 75-106803

ISBN 0-691-01751-4

PRINTED IN THE UNITED STATES OF AMERICA BY PRINCETON UNIVERSITY PRESS AT PRINCETON, NEW JERSEY

EDITORIAL NOTE *

This volume contains two long and important essays which reveal the main dynamic models Jung has used and developed over a period that began when he broke away from psychoanalysis and formulated his own concepts as distinct from those of Freud.

The first work, "On Psychic Energy," was written by Jung in answer to criticisms of his libido theory as it had been expounded in *Wandlungen und Symbole der Libido* (trans. as *Psychology of the Unconscious*) and *The Theory of Psychoanalysis*. Originally entitled "The Theory of Libido," it was begun *circa* 1912 but not completed till many years later (1928). Its importance lies in the clarity of its argument and the comprehensiveness of its subject-matter.

Another and longer essay, "On the Nature of the Psyche" (first version, 1946), presents an extensive review of Jung's theoretical position many years later and covers almost the whole field of his endeavour. In it the author thoroughly examines the concepts of consciousness and the unconscious against their historical background, particularly in relation to instinct, and elaborates his theory of archetypes, a subject first broached more than twenty-five years earlier in "Instinct and the Unconscious" (1919).

*

This paperback edition comprises two of eighteen essays in Volume 8 of the *Collected Works*. The paragraph numbers of the collected edition have been retained to facilitate reference, some essential corrections have been made (including revisions from the second edition of Volume 8), and a new index has been prepared. The bibliography includes only works relevant to this selection.

* From Volume 8 of the *Collected Works*. Material unrelated to the present selection has been omitted.

TABLE OF CONTENTS

EDITORIAL NOTE   V

I

On Psychic Energy   3
Translated from "Über die Energetik der Seele," in *Über
psychische Energetik und das Wesen der Träume* (Zurich:
Rascher, 1948).

I. General Remarks on the Energic Point of View in   3
    Psychology

    a. Introduction, 3
    b. The Possibility of Quantitative Measurement in
        Psychology, 6

II. Application of the Energic Standpoint   14

    a. The Psychological Concept of Energy, 14
    b. The Conservation of Energy, 18
    c. Entropy, 25
    d. Energism and Dynamism, 28

III. Fundamental Concepts of the Libido Theory   32

    a. Progression and Regression, 32
    b. Extraversion and Introversion, 40
    c. The Canalization of Libido, 41
    d. Symbol Formation, 45

IV. The Primitive Conception of Libido   61

I I

On the Nature of the Psyche 67

Translated from "Theoretische Überlegungen zum Wesen des Psychischen," *Von den Wurzeln des Bewusstseins* (Zurich: Rascher, 1954).

1. The Unconscious in Historical Perspective 69
2. The Significance of the Unconscious in Psychology 77
3. The Dissociability of the Psyche 83
4. Instinct and Will 88
5. Conscious and Unconscious 94
6. The Unconscious as a Multiple Consciousness 100
7. Patterns of Behaviour and Archetypes 110
8. General Considerations and Prospects 126
   Supplement 136

BIBLIOGRAPHY 147

INDEX 157

I

ON PSYCHIC ENERGY

ON PSYCHIC ENERGY [1]

I. GENERAL REMARKS ON THE ENERGIC
POINT OF VIEW IN PSYCHOLOGY

a. *Introduction*

1   The concept of libido which I have advanced [2] has met with many misunderstandings and, in some quarters, complete repudiation; it may therefore not be amiss if I examine once more the bases of this concept.

2   It is a generally recognized truth that physical events can be looked at in two ways: from the mechanistic and from the energic standpoint.[3] The mechanistic view is purely causal; it

---

[1] [First published as "Über die Energetik der Seele" in a volume of the same title (Zurich, 1928), which version was translated by H. G. and C. F. Baynes as "On Psychical Energy" in *Contributions to Analytical Psychology* (London and New York, 1928). The translators' foreword to the latter volume states that this paper "was framed soon after the author had finished the *Psychology of the Unconscious* [i.e., *Wandlungen und Symbole der Libido*, pub. 1912]. It was, however, pressed aside by the greater importance of the type-problem . . . , and, originally entitled 'The Theory of the Libido,' was taken up again only last summer." The original version was republished, under the same title, in *Über psychische Energetik und das Wesen der Träume* (Zurich, 1948). Both Swiss volumes are no. II of the Psychologische Abhandlungen.—EDITORS.]

[2] Cf. *Symbols of Transformation*, pars. 190ff.

[3] Cf. Wundt, *Grundzüge der physiologischen Psychologie*, III, 692ff. For the dynamistic standpoint see von Hartmann, *Weltanschauung der modernen Physik*, pp. 202ff.

conceives an event as the effect of a cause, in the sense that un-changing substances change their relations to one another according to fixed laws.

3   The energic point of view on the other hand is in essence final; [4] the event is traced back from effect to cause on the assumption that some kind of energy underlies the changes in phenomena, that it maintains itself as a constant throughout these changes and finally leads to entropy, a condition of general equilibrium. The flow of energy has a definite direction (goal) in that it follows the gradient of potential in a way that cannot be reversed. The idea of energy is not that of a substance moved in space; it is a concept abstracted from relations of movement. The concept, therefore, is founded not on the substances themselves but on their relations, whereas the moving substance itself is the basis of the mechanistic view.

4   Both points of view are indispensable for understanding physical events and consequently enjoy general recognition. Meanwhile, their continued existence side by side has gradually given rise to a third conception which is mechanistic as well as energic—although, logically speaking, the advance from cause to effect, the progressive action of the cause, cannot at the same time be the retrogressive selection of a means to an end.[5] It is not possible to conceive that one and the same combination of events could be simultaneously causal and final, for

[4] I use the word "final" rather than "teleological" in order to avoid the mis-understanding that attaches to the common conception of teleology, namely that it contains the idea of an anticipated end or goal.

[5] "Final causes and mechanical causes are mutually exclusive, because a function having one meaning cannot at the same time be one with many meanings" (Wundt, p. 728). It seems to me inadmissible to speak of "final causes," since this is a hybrid concept born of the mixing of the causal and final points of view. For Wundt the causal sequence has two terms and one meaning, i.e., cause M and effect E, whereas the final sequence has three terms and several meanings, i.e., the positing of a goal A, the means M', and the achievement of the goal E'. This construction I hold also to be a hybrid product, in that the positing of a goal is a causally conceived complement of the real final sequence M'–E', which like-wise has two terms and one meaning. In so far as the final standpoint is only the reverse of the causal (Wundt), M'–E' is simply the causal sequence M–E seen in reverse. The principle of finality recognizes no cause posited at the beginning, for the final standpoint is not a causal one and therefore has no concept of a cause, just as the causal standpoint has no concept of a goal or of an end to be achieved.

the one determination excludes the other. There are in fact two different points of view, the one reversing the other; for the principle of finality is the logical reverse of the principle of causality. Finality is not only logically possible, it is also an indispensable explanatory principle, since no explanation of nature can be mechanistic only. If indeed our concepts were exclusively those of moving bodies in space, there would be only causal explanation; but we have also to deal conceptually with relations of movement, which require the energic standpoint.[6] If this were not so, there would have been no need to invent the concept of energy.

5   The predominance of one or the other point of view depends less upon the objective behaviour of things than upon the psychological attitude of the investigator and thinker. Empathy leads to the mechanistic view, abstraction to the energic view. Both these types are liable to commit the error of hypostatizing their principles because of the so-called objective facts of experience. They make the mistake of assuming that the subjective concept is identical with the behaviour of the thing itself; that, for example, causality as we experience it is also to be found objectively in the behaviour of things. This error is very common and leads to incessant conflicts with the opposing principle; for, as was said, it is impossible to think of the determining factor being both causal and final at the same time. But this intolerable contradiction only comes about through the illegitimate and thoughtless projection into the object of what is a mere point of view. Our points of view remain without contradiction only when they are restricted to the sphere of the psychological and are projected merely as hypotheses into the objective behaviour of things. The causality principle can suffer without contradiction its logical reversal, but the facts cannot; hence causality and finality must preclude one another in the object. On the well-known principle of minimizing differences, it is customary to effect a theoretically inadmissible

[6] The conflict between energism and mechanism is a parallel of the old problem of universals. Certainly it is true that the individual thing is all that is "given" in sense perception, and to that extent a universal is only a *nomen*, a word. But at the same time the similarities, the relations between things, are also given, and to that extent a universal is a reality (Abelard's "relative realism").

compromise by regarding a process as partly causal, partly final [7]—a compromise which gives rise to all sorts of theoretical hybrids but which yields, it cannot be denied, a relatively faithful picture of reality.[8] We must always bear in mind that despite the most beautiful agreement between the facts and our ideas, explanatory principles are only points of view, that is, manifestations of the psychological attitude and of the *a priori* conditions under which all thinking takes place.

b. The Possibility of Quantitative Measurement in Psychology

6   From what has been said it should be sufficiently clear that every event requires the mechanistic-causal as well as the energic-final point of view. Expediency, that is to say, the possibility of obtaining results, alone decides whether the one or the other view is to be preferred. If, for example, the qualitative side of the event comes into question, then the energic point of view takes second place, because it has nothing to do with the things themselves but only with their quantitative relations of movement.

7   It has been much disputed whether or not mental and psychic events can be subjected to an energic view. *A priori* there is no reason why this should not be possible, since there are no grounds for excluding psychic events from the field of objective experience. The psyche itself can very well be an object of experience. Yet, as Wundt's example shows,[9] one can question in good faith whether the energic point of view is applicable to psychic phenomena at all, and if it is applicable, whether the psyche can be looked upon as a relatively closed system.

[7] Finality and causality are two possible ways of understanding which form an antinomy. They are progressive and regressive "interpretants" (Wundt) and as such are contradictory. Naturally this statement is correct only if it is assumed that the concept of energy is an abstraction that expresses relation. ("Energy is relation": von Hartmann, p. 196). But the statement is not correct if an hypostatized concept of energy is assumed, as in Ostwald's *Die Philosophie der Werte*.
[8] "The difference between the teleological and the causal view of things is not a real one dividing the contents of experience into two disparate realms. The sole difference between the two views is the formal one that a causal connection belongs as a complement to every final relationship, and conversely, every causal connection can be given, if need be, a teleological form." Wundt, p. 737.
[9] [Cf. n. 5.—EDITORS.]

8   As to the first point, I am in entire agreement with von Grot
—one of the first to propose the concept of psychic energy—when
he says: "The concept of psychic energy is as much justified in
science as that of physical energy, and psychic energy has just as
many quantitative measurements and different forms as has
physical energy." [10]

9   As to the second point, I differ from previous investigators in
that I am not concerned in the least in fitting psychic energy
processes into the physical system. I am not interested in such a
classification because we have at best only the vaguest con-
jectures to go on and no real point of departure. Although it
seems certain to me that psychic energy is in some way or other
closely connected with physical processes, yet, in order to speak
with any authority about this connection, we would need quite
different experiences and insights. As to the philosophical side
of the question, I entirely endorse the views of Busse.[11] I must
also support Külpe when he says: "It would thus make no
difference whether a quantum of mental energy inserts itself
into the course of the material process or not: the law of the
conservation of energy as formulated hitherto would not be
impaired." [12]

10   In my view the psychophysical relation is a problem in itself,
which perhaps will be solved some day. In the meantime, however, the psychologist need not be held up by this difficulty, but
can regard the psyche as a *relatively* closed system. In that case
we must certainly break with what seems to me the untenable
"psychophysical" hypothesis, since its epiphenomenalist point
of view is simply a legacy from the old-fashioned scientific materialism. Thus, as Lasswitz, von Grot, and others think, the
phenomena of consciousness have no functional connections
with one another, for they are *only* (!) "phenomena, expressions,
symptoms of certain deeper functional relationships." The
causal connections existing between psychic facts, which we can
observe at any time, contradict the epiphenomenon theory,
which has a fatal similarity to the materialistic belief that the
psyche is secreted by the brain as the gall is by the liver. A

10 "Die Begriffe der Seele und der psychischen Energie in der Psychologie,"
Archiv für systematische Philosophie, IV.
11 Busse, *Geist und Körper, Seele und Leib.*
12 Külpe, *Einleitung in die Philosophie,* p. 150.

psychology that treats the psyche as an epiphenomenon would better call itself brain-psychology, and remain satisfied with the meagre results that such a psycho-physiology can yield. The psyche deserves to be taken as a phenomenon in its own right; there are no grounds at all for regarding it as a mere epiphenomenon, dependent though it may be on the functioning of the brain. One would be as little justified in regarding life as an epiphenomenon of the chemistry of carbon compounds.

11   The immediate experience of quantitative psychic relations on the one hand, and the unfathomable nature of a psychophysical connection on the other, justify at least a provisional view of the psyche as a relatively closed system. Here I find myself in direct opposition to von Grot's psychophysical energetics. In my view he is moving here on very uncertain ground, so that his further remarks have little plausibility. Nevertheless, I would like to put von Grot's formulations before the reader in his own words, as they represent the opinions of a pioneer in this difficult field:

(1) Psychic energies possess quantity and mass, just like physical energies.

(2) As different forms of psychic work and psychic potentiality, they can be transformed into one another.

(3) They can be converted into physical energies and vice versa, by means of physiological processes.[13]

12   I need scarcely add that statement three seems to require a significant question mark. In the last analysis it is only expediency that can decide, not whether the energic view is possible in itself, but whether it promises results in practice.[14]

13   The possibility of exact quantitative measurement of physical energy has *proved* that the energic standpoint does yield results when applied to physical events. But it would still be possible to consider physical events as forms of energy even if there were no exact quantitative measurement but merely the possibility of *estimating quantities*.[15] If, however, even that

13 Ibid., p. 323.

14 Von Grot goes so far as to say (p. 324): "The burden of proof falls on those who deny psychic energy, not on those who acknowledge it."

15 This was actually the case with Descartes, who first formulated the principle of the conservation of the quantity of movement, but had not at his disposal the methods of physical measurement which were discovered only in recent times.

proved to be impossible, then the energic point of view would have to be abandoned, since if there is not at least a possibility of a quantitative estimate the energic standpoint is quite superfluous.

(i) THE SUBJECTIVE SYSTEM OF VALUES

14 The applicability of the energic standpoint to psychology rests, then, exclusively on the question whether a quantitative estimate of psychic energy is possible or not. This question can be met with an unconditional affirmative, since our psyche actually possesses an extraordinarily well-developed evaluating system, namely the *system of psychological values*. Values are quantitative estimates of energy. Here it should be remarked that in our collective moral and aesthetic values we have at our disposal not merely an objective system of value but an objective system of measurement. This system of measurement is not, however, directly available for our purpose, since it is a general scale of values which takes account only indirectly of subjective, that is to say individual, psychological conditions.

15 What we must first of all consider, therefore, is the *subjective value system,* the subjective estimates of the single individual. We can, as a matter of fact, estimate the subjective values of our psychic contents up to a certain point, even though it is at times extraordinarily difficult to measure them with objective accuracy against the generally established values. However, this comparison is superfluous for our purpose, as already said. We can weigh our subjective evaluations against one another and determine their *relative* strength. Their measurement is nevertheless relative to the value of other contents and therefore not absolute and objective, but it is sufficient for our purpose inasmuch as different intensities of value in relation to similar qualities can be recognized with certainty, while equal values under the same conditions plainly maintain themselves in equilibrium.

16 The difficulty begins only when we have to compare the value intensities of different qualities, say the value of a scientific idea compared with a feeling impression. Here the subjective estimate becomes uncertain and therefore unreliable. In the same way, the subjective estimate is restricted to the contents

of consciousness; hence it is useless with respect to unconscious influences, where we are concerned with valuations that go beyond the boundaries of consciousness.

17   In view of the compensatory relationship known to exist between the conscious and the unconscious,[16] however, it is of great importance to find a way of determining the value of unconscious products. If we want to carry through the energic approach to psychic events, we must bear in mind the exceedingly important fact that conscious values can apparently disappear without showing themselves again in an equivalent conscious achievement. In this case we should theoretically expect their appearance in the unconscious. But since the unconscious is not directly accessible either in ourselves or in others, the evaluation can only be an indirect one, so we must have recourse to auxiliary methods in order to arrive at our estimates of value. In the case of subjective evaluation, feeling and insight come to our aid immediately, because these are functions which have been developing over long periods of time and have become very finely differentiated. Even the child practises very early the differentiation of his scale of values; he weighs up whether he likes his father or mother better, who comes in the second and third place, who is most hated, etc. This conscious evaluation not only breaks down in regard to the manifestations of the unconscious but is actually twisted into the most obvious false estimates, also described as "repressions" or the "displacement of affect." Subjective evaluation is therefore completely out of the question in estimating unconscious value intensities. Consequently we need an objective point of departure that will make an indirect but objective estimate possible.

(ii) OBJECTIVE ESTIMATE OF QUANTITY

18   In my study of the phenomena of association [17] I have shown that there are certain constellations of psychic elements grouped

[16] The one-sidedness of consciousness is compensated by a counterposition in the unconscious. It is chiefly the facts of psychopathology that show the compensatory attitude of the unconscious most clearly. Evidence for this may be found in the writings of Freud and Adler, also in my "Psychology of Dementia Praecox." For a theoretical discussion see my "Instinct and the Unconscious," pars. 263ff., infra. On the general significance of psychological compensation see Maeder, "Régulation psychique et guérison."

[17] [Cf. Vol. 2, Collected Works (1918 edn.: Studies in Word Association).—EDITORS.]

round feeling-toned [18] contents, which I have called "complexes." The feeling-toned content, the complex, consists of a nuclear element and a large number of secondarily constellated associations. The nuclear element consists of two components: first, a factor determined by experience and causally related to the environment; second, a factor innate in the individual's character and determined by his disposition.

19   The nuclear element is characterized by its feeling-tone, the emphasis resulting from the intensity of affect. This emphasis, expressed in terms of energy, is a value quantity. In so far as the nuclear element is conscious, the quantity can be subjectively estimated, at least relatively. But if, as frequently happens, the nuclear element is unconscious,[19] at any rate in its psychological significance, then a subjective estimate becomes impossible, and one must substitute the indirect method of evaluation. This is based, in principle, on the following fact:

[18] [Cf. *Psychiatric Studies,* par. 168, n. 2a.—EDITORS.]

[19] That a complex or its essential nucleus can be unconscious is not a self-evident fact. A complex would not be a complex at all if it did not possess a certain, even a considerable, affective intensity. One would expect that this energic value would automatically force the complex into consciousness, that the power of attraction inherent within it would compel conscious attention. (Fields of power attract one another mutually!) That this, as experience shows, is frequently not the case requires a special explanation. The readiest and simplest explanation is given by Freud's theory of repression. This theory presupposes a counterposition in the conscious mind: the conscious attitude is, so to speak, hostile to the unconscious complex and does not allow it to reach consciousness. This theory certainly explains very many cases, but in my experience there are some cases that cannot be so explained. Actually, the repression theory takes account only of those cases in which a content, in itself perfectly capable of becoming conscious, is either quite consciously repressed and made unconscious, or has right from the beginning never reached consciousness. It does not take into account those other cases in which a content of high energic intensity is formed out of unconscious material that is not in itself capable of becoming conscious, and so cannot be made conscious at all, or only with the greatest difficulty. In these cases the conscious attitude, far from being hostile to the unconscious content, would be most favourably disposed towards it, as in the case of creative products, which, as we know, almost always have their first beginnings in the unconscious. Just as a mother awaits her child with longing and yet brings it into the world only with effort and pain, so a new, creative content, despite the willingness of the conscious mind, can remain for a long time in the unconscious without being "repressed." Though it has a high energic value it still does not become conscious. Cases of this sort are not too difficult to explain. Because the content is new and therefore strange to consciousness, there are no existing

that the nuclear element automatically creates a complex to the degree that it is affectively toned and possesses energic value, as I have shown in detail in the second and third chapters of my "Psychology of Dementia Praecox." The nuclear element has a constellating power corresponding to its energic value. It produces a specific constellation of psychic contents, thus giving rise to the complex, which is a constellation of psychic contents dynamically conditioned by the energic value. The resultant constellation, however, is not just an irradiation of the psychic stimulus, but a selection of the stimulated psychic contents which is conditioned by the *quality* of the nuclear element. This selection cannot, of course, be explained in terms of energy, because the energic explanation is quantitative and not qualitative. For a qualitative explanation we must have recourse to the causal view.[20] The proposition upon which the objective estimate of psychological value intensities is based therefore runs as follows: *the constellating power of the nuclear element corresponds to its value intensity, i.e., to its energy.*

20   But what means have we of estimating the energic value of the constellating power which enriches the complex with associations? We can estimate this quantum of energy in various ways: (1) from the relative number of constellations effected by the nuclear element; (2) from the relative frequency and intensity of the reactions indicating a disturbance or complex; (3) from the intensity of the accompanying affects.

21   1. The data required to determine the relative number of constellations may be obtained partly by direct observation and partly by analytical deduction. That is to say, the more frequent the constellations conditioned by one and the same complex, the greater must be its psychological valency.

22   2. The reactions indicating a disturbance or complex do not

associations and connecting bridges to the conscious contents. All these connections must first be laid down with considerable effort, for without them no consciousness is possible. Two main grounds must therefore be considered in explaining the unconsciousness of a complex: (1) the repression of a content capable of becoming conscious, and (2) the strangeness of a content not yet capable of reaching consciousness.

20 Or to an hypostatized concept of energy, such as Ostwald holds. But the concept of substance needed for a causal-mechanistic mode of explanation can hardly be circumvented in this fashion, since "energy" is at bottom always a concept concerned with quantity alone.

include only the symptoms that appear in the course of the association experiment. These are really nothing but the effects of the complex, and their form is determined by the particular type of experiment. We are more concerned here with those phenomena that are peculiar to psychological processes outside experimental conditions. Freud has described the greater part of them under the head of lapses of speech, mistakes in writing, slips of memory, misunderstandings, and other symptomatic actions. To these we must add the automatisms described by me, "thought-deprivation," "interdiction," "irrelevant talk," [21] etc. As I have shown in my association experiments, the intensity of these phenomena can be directly determined by a time record, and the same thing is possible also in the case of an unrestricted psychological procedure, when, watch in hand, we can easily determine the value intensity from the time taken by the patient to speak about certain things. It might be objected that patients very often waste the better part of their time talking about irrelevancies in order to evade the main issue, but that only shows how much more important these so-called irrelevancies are to them. The observer must guard against arbitrary judgments that explain the real interests of the patient as irrelevant, in accordance with some subjective, theoretical assumption of the analyst's. In determining values, he must hold strictly to objective criteria. Thus, if a patient wastes hours complaining about her servants instead of coming to the main conflict, which may have been gauged quite correctly by the analyst, this only means that the servant-complex has in fact a higher energic value than the still unconscious conflict, which will perhaps reveal itself as the nuclear element only during the further course of treatment, or that the inhibition exercised by the highly valued conscious position keeps the nuclear element in the unconscious through overcompensation.

23   3. In order to determine the intensity of affective phenomena we have objective methods which, while not measuring the quantity of affect, nevertheless permit an estimate. Experimental psychology has furnished us with a number of such methods. Apart from time measurements, which determine the inhibition

21 [Cf. "The Psychology of Dementia Praecox," pars. 175ff.—EDITORS.]

of the association process rather than the actual affects, we have the following devices in particular:

    (a) the pulse curve; [22]
    (b) the respiration curve; [23]
    (c) the psycho-galvanic phenomenon. [24]

[24] The easily recognizable changes in these curves permit inferential estimates to be made concerning the intensity of the disturbing cause. It is also possible, as experience has shown to our satisfaction, deliberately to induce affective phenomena in the subject by means of psychological stimuli which one knows to be especially charged with affect for this particular individual in relation to the experimenter. [25]

[25] Besides these experimental methods we have a highly differentiated subjective system for recognizing and evaluating affective phenomena in others. There is present in each of us a direct instinct for registering this, which animals also possess in high degree, with respect not only to their own species but also to other animals and human beings. We can perceive the slightest emotional fluctuations in others and have a very fine feeling for the quality and quantity of affects in our fellow-men.

II. APPLICATION OF THE ENERGIC STANDPOINT

a. The Psychological Concept of Energy

[26] The term "psychic energy" has long been in use. We find it, for example, as early as Schiller,[26] and the energic point of view

[22] Cf. Berger, *Über die körperlichen Aeusserungen psychischer Zustände;* Lehmann, *Die körperlichen Äusserungen psychischer Zustände,* trans. (into German) by Bendixen.

[23] Peterson and Jung, "Psycho-physical Investigations with the Galvanometer and Pneumograph in Normal and Insane Individuals"; Nunberg, "On the Physical Accompaniments of Association Processes," in Jung, *Studies in Word Association;* Ricksher and Jung, "Further Investigations on the Galvanic Phenomenon."

[24] Veraguth, *Das psycho-galvanische Reflexphänomen;* Binswanger, "On the Psycho-galvanic Phenomenon in Association Experiments," in Jung, *Studies in Word Association.*

[25] Cf. *Studies in Word Association* and "The Association Method."

[26] Schiller thinks in terms of energy, so to speak. He operates with ideas like "transfer of intensity," etc. Cf. *On the Aesthetic Education of Man,* trans. by Snell.

was also used by von Grot [27] and Theodor Lipps.[28] Lipps distinguishes psychic energy from physical energy, while Stern [29] leaves the question of their connection open. We have to thank Lipps for the distinction between psychic *energy* and psychic *force*. For Lipps, psychic force is the possibility of processes arising in the psyche at all and of attaining a certain degree of efficiency. Psychic energy, on the other hand, is defined by Lipps as the "inherent capacity of these processes to actualize this force in themselves." [30] Elsewhere Lipps speaks of "psychic quantities." The distinction between force and energy is a conceptual necessity, for energy is really a concept and, as such, does not exist objectively in the phenomena themselves but only in the specific data of experience. In other words, energy is always experienced specifically as motion and force when actual, and as a state or condition when potential. Psychic energy appears, when actual, in the specific, dynamic phenomena of the psyche, such as instinct, wishing, willing, affect, attention, capacity for work, etc., which make up the psychic forces. When potential, energy shows itself in specific achievements, possibilities, aptitudes, attitudes, etc., which are its various states.

[27] The differentiation of specific energies, such as pleasure energy, sensation energy, contrary energy, etc., proposed by Lipps, seems to me theoretically inadmissible as the specific forms of energy are the above-mentioned forces and states. Energy is a quantitative concept which includes them all. It is only these forces and states that are determined qualitatively, for they are concepts that express qualities brought into action through energy. The concept of quantity should never be qualitative at the same time, otherwise it would never enable us to expound the relations between forces, which is after all its real function.

[28] Since, unfortunately, we cannot prove scientifically that a relation of equivalence exists between physical and psychic energy,[31] we have no alternative except either to drop the

27 "Die Begriffe der Seele und der psychischen Energie in der Psychologie."
28 *Leitfaden der Psychologie,* pp. 62, 66f.
29 Stern, *Über Psychologie der individuellen Differenzen,* pp. 119ff.
30 *Leitfaden der Psychologie,* p. 36 (1903 edn.).
31 Maeder is of the opinion that the "creative activity" of the organism, and particularly that of the psyche, "exceeds the energy consumed." He also holds that

energetic viewpoint altogether, or else to postulate a special psychic energy—which would be entirely possible as a hypothetical operation. Psychology as much as physics may avail itself of the right to build its own concepts, as Lipps has already remarked, but only in so far as the energic view proves its value and is not just a summing-up under a vague general concept—an objection justly enough raised by Wundt. We are of the opinion, however, that the energic view of psychic phenomena is a valuable one because it enables us to recognize just those quantitative relations whose existence in the psyche cannot possibly be denied but which are easily overlooked from a purely qualitative standpoint.

29   Now if the psyche consisted, as the psychologists of the conscious mind maintain, of conscious processes alone (admittedly somewhat "dark" now and then), we might rest content with the postulate of a "special psychic energy." But since we are persuaded that the unconscious processes also belong to psychology, and not merely to the physiology of the brain (as substratum processes), we are obliged to put our concept of energy on a rather broader basis. We fully agree with Wundt that there are things of which we are dimly conscious. We accept, as he does, a scale of clarity for conscious contents, but for us the psyche does not stop where the blackness begins but is continued right into the unconscious. We also leave brain-psychology its share, since we assume that the unconscious functions ultimately go over into substratum processes to which no psychic quality can be assigned, except by way of the philosophical hypothesis of pan-psychism.

30   In delimiting a concept of psychic energy we are thus faced with certain difficulties, because we have absolutely no means of dividing what is psychic from the biological process as such. Biology as much as psychology can be approached from the energic standpoint, in so far as the biologist feels it to be useful and valuable. Like the psyche, the life-process in general does not stand in any exactly demonstrable relationship of equivalence to physical energy.

---

in regard to the psyche, together with the principle of conservation and the principle of entropy, one must make use of yet a third principle, that of integration. Cf. *Heilung und Entwicklung im Seelenleben*, pp. 50 and 69f.

31   If we take our stand on the basis of scientific common sense
and avoid philosophical considerations which would carry us
too far, we would probably do best to regard the psychic process
simply as a life-process. In this way we enlarge the narrower
concept of psychic energy to a broader one of life-energy, which
includes "psychic energy" as a specific part. We thus gain the
advantage of being able to follow quantitative relations beyond
the narrow confines of the psychic into the sphere of biological
functions in general, and so can do justice, if need be, to the long
discussed and ever-present problem of "mind and body."

32   The concept of life-energy has nothing to do with a so-called
life-force, for this, *qua* force, would be nothing more than a
specific form of universal energy. To regard life-energy thus,
and so bridge over the still yawning gulf between physical
processes and life-processes, would be to do away with the special
claims of bio-energetics as opposed to physical energetics. I have
therefore suggested that, in view of the psychological use we
intend to make of it, we call our hypothetical life-energy
"libido." To this extent I have differentiated it from a concept
of universal energy, so maintaining the right of biology and psychology to form their own concepts. In adopting this usage I do
not in any way wish to forestall workers in the field of bio-
energetics, but freely admit that I have adopted the term libido
with the intention of using it for *our* purposes: for theirs, some
such term as "bio-energy" or "vital energy" may be preferred.

33   I must at this point guard against a possible misunderstanding. I have not the smallest intention, in the present paper, of
letting myself in for a discussion of the controversial question of
psychophysical parallelism and reciprocal action. These theories
are speculations concerning the possibility of mind and body
functioning together or side by side, and they touch on the
very point I am purposely leaving out of account here, namely
whether the psychic energy process exists independently of, or
is included in, the physical process. In my view we know practically nothing about this. Like Busse,[32] I consider the idea of
reciprocal action tenable, and can see no reason to prejudice its
credibility with the hypothesis of psychophysical parallelism. To
the psychotherapist, whose special field lies just in this crucial

32 *Geist und Körper, Seele und Leib.*

sphere of the interaction of mind and body, it seems highly probable that the psychic and the physical are not two independent
parallel processes, but are essentially connected through reciprocal action, although the actual nature of this relationship is
still completely outside our experience. Exhaustive discussions
of this question may be all very well for philosophers, but
empirical psychology should confine itself to empirically accessible facts. Even though we have not yet succeeded in proving
that the processes of psychic energy are included in the physical
process, the opponents of such a possibility have been equally
unsuccessful in separating the psychic from the physical with
any certainty.

b. The Conservation of Energy

34   If we undertake to view the psychic life-process from the
energic standpoint, we must not rest content with the mere
concept, but must accept the obligation to test its applicability
to empirical material. An energic standpoint is otiose if its
main principle, the conservation of energy, proves to be inap-
plicable. Here we must follow Busse's suggestion and distinguish
between the principle of equivalence and the principle of constancy.[33] The principle of equivalence states that "for a given
quantity of energy expended or consumed in bringing about a
certain condition, an equal quantity of the same or another
form of energy will appear elsewhere"; while the principle of
constancy states that "the sum total of energy remains constant,
and is susceptible neither of increase nor of decrease." Hence
the principle of constancy is a logically necessary but generalized
conclusion from the principle of equivalence and is not so important in practice, since our experience is always concerned
with partial systems only.

35   For our purpose, the principle of equivalence is the only one
of immediate concern. In my book *Symbols of Transformation*,[34] I have demonstrated the possibility of considering certain
developmental processes and other transformations of the kind
under the principle of equivalence. I will not repeat *in extenso*
what I have said there, but will only emphasize once again that

[33] Ibid.   [34] Cf. particularly Part II, ch. III.

Freud's investigation of sexuality has made many valuable contributions to our problem. Nowhere can we see more clearly than in the relation of sexuality to the total psyche how the disappearance of a given quantum of libido is followed by the appearance of an equivalent value in another form. Unfortunately Freud's very understandable over-valuation of sexuality led him to reduce transformations of other specific psychic forces co-ordinated with sexuality to sexuality pure and simple, thus bringing upon himself the not unjustified charge of pansexualism. The defect of the Freudian view lies in the onesidedness to which the mechanistic-causal standpoint always inclines, that is to say in the all-simplifying *reductio ad causam,* which, the truer, the simpler, the more inclusive it is, does the less justice to the product thus analysed and reduced. Anyone who reads Freud's works with attention will see what an important role the equivalence principle plays in the structure of his theories. This can be seen particularly clearly in his investigations of case material, where he gives an account of repressions and their substitute formations.[35] Anyone who has had practical experience of this field knows that the equivalence principle is of great heuristic value in the treatment of neuroses. Even if its application is not always conscious, you nevertheless apply it instinctively or by feeling. For instance, when a conscious value, say a transference, decreases or actually disappears, you immediately look for the substitute formation, expecting to see an equivalent value spring up somewhere else. It is not difficult to find the substitute if the substitute formation is a conscious content, but there are frequent cases where a sum of libido disappears apparently without forming a substitute. In that case the substitute is unconscious, or, as usually happens, the patient is unaware that some new psychic fact is the corresponding substitute formation. But it may also happen that a considerable sum of libido disappears as though completely swallowed up by the unconscious, with no new value appearing in its stead. In such cases it is advisable to cling firmly to the principle of equivalence, for careful observation of the patient will soon reveal signs of unconscious activity, for instance an intensification of certain symptoms, or a new symptom, or

---

[35] *Sammlung kleiner Schriften zur Neurosenlehre* [cf. *Collected Papers,* I–IV].

peculiar dreams, or strange, fleeting fragments of fantasy, etc. If the analyst succeeds in bringing these hidden contents into consciousness, it can usually be shown that the libido which disappeared from consciousness generated a product in the unconscious which, despite all differences, has not a few features in common with the conscious contents that lost their energy. It is as if the libido dragged with it into the unconscious certain qualities which are often so distinct that one can recognize from their character the source of the libido now activating the unconscious.

36   There are many striking and well-known examples of these transformations. For instance, when a child begins to separate himself subjectively from his parents, fantasies of substitute parents arise, and these fantasies are almost always transferred to real people. Transferences of this sort prove untenable in the long run, because the maturing personality must assimilate the parental complex and achieve authority, responsibility, and independence. He or she must become a father or mother. Another field rich in striking examples is the psychology of Christianity, where the repression of instincts (i.e., of primitive instinctuality) leads to religious substitute formations, such as the medieval *Gottesminne*, 'love of God,' the sexual character of which only the blind could fail to see.

37   These reflections lead us to a further analogy with the theory of physical energy. As we know, the theory of energy recognizes not only a factor of *intensity*, but also a factor of *extensity*, the latter being a necessary addition in practice to the pure concept of energy. It combines the concept of pure intensity with the concept of quantity (e.g., the quantity of light as opposed to its strength). "The quantity, or the extensity factor, of energy is attached to one structure and cannot be transferred to another structure without carrying with it parts of the first; but the intensity factor can pass from one structure to another." [36] The extensity factor, therefore, shows the dynamic measure of energy present at any time in a given phenomenon. [37]

38   Similarly, there is a psychological extensity factor which cannot pass into a new structure without carrying over parts or characteristics of the previous structure with which it was con-

[36] Hartmann, *Weltanschauung der modernen Physik*, p. 6.

[37] Physics today equates energy with mass, but this is irrelevant for our purpose.

nected. In my earlier work, I have drawn particular attention to this peculiarity of energy transformation, and have shown that libido does not leave a structure as pure intensity and pass without trace into another, but that it takes the character of the old function over into the new.[38] This peculiarity is so striking that it gives rise to false conclusions—not only to wrong theories, but to self-deceptions fraught with unfortunate consequences. For instance, say a sum of libido having a certain sexual form passes over into another structure, taking with it some of the peculiarities of its previous application. It is then very tempting to think that the dynamism of the new structure will be sexual too.[39] Or it may be that the libido of some spiritual activity goes over into an essentially material interest, whereupon the individual erroneously believes that the new structure is equally spiritual in character. These conclusions are false in principle because they take only the relative similarities of the two structures into account while ignoring their equally essential differences.

39   Practical experience teaches us as a general rule that a psychic activity can find a substitute only on the basis of equivalence. A pathological interest, for example, an intense attachment to a symptom, can be replaced only by an equally intense attachment to another interest, which is why a release of libido from the symptom never takes place without this substitute. If the substitute is of less energic value, we know at once that a part of the energy is to be sought elsewhere—if not in the conscious mind, then in unconscious fantasy formations or in a disturbance of the "parties supérieures" of the psychological functions (to borrow an apt expression of Janet's).

40   Apart from these practical experiences which have long been at our disposal, the energic point of view also enables us to

---

38 *Symbols of Transformation,* par. 226.
39 The reduction of a complex structure to sexuality is a valid causal explanation only if it is agreed beforehand that we are interested in explaining solely the function of the sexual components in complex structures. But if we accept the reduction to sexuality as valid, this can only be done on the tacit assumption that we are dealing with an exclusively sexual structure. To assume this, however, is to assert *a priori* that a complex psychic structure can only be a sexual structure, a manifest *petitio principii!* It cannot be asserted that sexuality is the only fundamental psychic instinct, hence every explanation on a sexual basis can be only a partial explanation, never an all-sufficing psychological theory.

build up another side of our theory. According to the causal standpoint of Freud, there exists only this same immutable substance, the sexual component, to whose activity every interpretation is led back with monotonous regularity, a fact which Freud himself once pointed out. It is obvious that the spirit of the *reductio ad causam* or *reductio in primam figuram* can never do justice to the idea of final development, of such paramount importance in psychology, because each change in the conditions is seen as nothing but a "sublimation" of the basic substance and therefore as a masked expression of the same old thing.

41   The idea of development is possible only if the concept of an immutable substance is not hypostatized by appeals to a so-called "objective reality"—that is to say, if causality is not assumed to be identical with the behaviour of things. The idea of development requires the possibility of change in substances, which, from the energic standpoint, appear as systems of energy capable of theoretically unlimited interchangeability and modulation under the principle of equivalence, and on the obvious assumption of a difference in potential. Here again, just as in examining the relations between causality and finality, we come upon an insoluble antinomy resulting from an illegitimate projection of the energic hypothesis, for an immutable substance cannot at the same time be a system of energy.[40] According to the mechanistic view, energy is attached to substance, so that Wundt can speak of an "energy of the psychic" which has increased in the course of time and therefore does not permit the application of the principles of energy. From the energic standpoint, on the other hand, substance is nothing more than the expression or sign of an energic system. This antinomy is insoluble only so long as it is forgotten that points of view correspond to fundamental psychological attitudes, which obviously coincide to some extent with the conditions and behaviour of objects—a coincidence that renders the points of view applicable in practice. It is therefore quite understandable that causalists and finalists alike should fight desperately for the objective validity of their principles, since the principle each is defending is also that of his personal attitude to life and the

---

[40] This applies only to the macrophysical realm, where "absolute" laws hold good.

world, and no one will allow without protest that his attitude may have only a conditional validity. This unwelcome admission feels somewhat like a suicidal attempt to saw off the branch upon which one is sitting. But the unavoidable antinomies to which the projection of logically justified principles gives rise force us to a fundamental examination of our own psychological attitudes, for only in this way can we avoid doing violence to the other logically valid principle. The antinomy must resolve itself in an *antinomian postulate,* however unsatisfactory this may be to our concretistic thinking, and however sorely it afflicts the spirit of natural science to admit that the essence of so-called reality is of a mysterious irrationality. This, however, necessarily follows from an acceptance of the antinomian postulate.[41]

42   The theory of development cannot do without the final point of view. Even Darwin, as Wundt points out, worked with final concepts, such as adaptation. The palpable fact of differentiation and development can never be explained exhaustively by causality; it requires also the final point of view, which man produced in the course of his psychic evolution, as he also produced the causal.

43   According to the concept of finality, causes are understood as means to an end. A simple example is the process of regression. Regarded causally, regression is determined, say, by a "mother fixation." But from the final standpoint the libido regresses to the *imago* of the mother in order to find there the memory associations by means of which further development can take place, for instance from a sexual system into an intellectual or spiritual system.

44   The first explanation exhausts itself in stressing the importance of the cause and completely overlooks the final significance of the regressive process. From this angle the whole edifice of civilization becomes a mere substitute for the impossibility of incest. But the second explanation allows us to foresee what will follow from the regression, and at the same time it helps us to understand the significance of the memory-images that have been reactivated by the regressive libido. To the causalist the latter interpretation naturally seems unbelievably hypothetical,

41 [Cf. *Psychological Types,* Def. 36: "Irrational."]

while to the finalist the "mother fixation" is an arbitrary assumption. This assumption, he objects, entirely fails to take note of the aim, which alone can be made responsible for the reactivation of the mother imago. Adler, for instance, raises numerous objections of this sort against Freud's theory. In my *Symbols of Transformation* I tried to do justice to both views, and met for my pains the accusation from both sides of holding an obscurantist and dubious position. In this I share the fate of neutrals in wartime, to whom even good faith is often denied.

45   What to the causal view is *fact* to the final view is *symbol,* and vice versa. Everything that is real and essential to the one is unreal and inessential to the other. We are therefore forced to resort to the antinomian postulate and must view the world, too, as a psychic phenomenon. Certainly it is necessary for science to know how things are "in themselves," but even science cannot escape the psychological conditions of knowledge, and psychology must be peculiarly alive to these conditions. Since the psyche also possesses the final point of view, it is psychologically inadmissible to adopt the purely causal attitude to psychic phenomena, not to mention the all too familiar monotony of its one-sided interpretations.

46   The symbolic interpretation of causes by means of the energic standpoint is necessary for the differentiation of the psyche, since unless the facts are symbolically interpreted, the causes remain immutable substances which go on operating continuously, as in the case of Freud's old trauma theory. Cause alone does not make development possible. For the psyche the *reductio ad causam* is the very reverse of development; it binds the libido to the elementary facts. From the standpoint of rationalism this is all that can be desired, but from the standpoint of the psyche it is lifeless and comfortless boredom—though it should never be forgotten that for many people it is absolutely necessary to keep their libido close to the basic facts. But, in so far as this requirement is fulfilled, the psyche cannot always remain on this level but must go on developing, the causes transforming themselves into means to an end, into symbolical expressions for the way that lies ahead. The exclusive importance of the cause, i.e., its energic value, thus disappears and emerges again in the symbol, whose power of attraction represents the equivalent quantum of libido. The energic value of

a cause is never abolished by positing an arbitrary and rational goal: that is always a makeshift.

47   Psychic development cannot be accomplished by intention and will alone; it needs the attraction of the symbol, whose value quantum exceeds that of the cause. But the formation of a symbol cannot take place until the mind has dwelt long enough on the elementary facts, that is to say until the inner or outer necessities of the life-process have brought about a transformation of energy. If man lived altogether instinctively and automatically, the transformation could come about in accordance with purely biological laws. We can still see something of the sort in the psychic life of primitives, which is entirely concretistic and entirely symbolical at once. In civilized man the rationalism of consciousness, otherwise so useful to him, proves to be a most formidable obstacle to the frictionless transformation of energy. Reason, always seeking to avoid what to it is an unbearable antinomy, takes its stand exclusively on one side or the other, and convulsively seeks to hold fast to the values it has once chosen. It will continue to do this so long as human reason passes for an "immutable substance," thereby precluding any symbolical view of itself. But reason is only relative, and eventually checks itself in its own antinomies. It too is only a means to an end, a symbolical expression for a transitional stage in the path of development.

c. Entropy

48   The principle of equivalence is one proposition of practical importance in the theory of energy; the other proposition, necessary and complementary, is the principle of entropy. Transformations of energy are possible only as a result of differences in intensity. According to Carnot's law, heat can be converted into work only by passing from a warmer to a colder body. But mechanical work is continually being converted into heat, which on account of its reduced intensity cannot be converted back into work. In this way a closed energic system gradually reduces its differences in intensity to an even temperature, whereby any further change is prohibited.

49   So far as our experience goes, the principle of entropy is known to us only as a principle of partial processes which make

up a relatively closed system. The psyche, too, can be regarded as such a relatively closed system, in which transformations of energy lead to an equalization of differences. According to Boltzmann's formulation,[42] this levelling process corresponds to a transition from an improbable to a probable state, whereby the possibility of further change is increasingly limited. Psychologically, we can see this process at work in the development of a lasting and relatively unchanging attitude. After violent oscillations at the beginning the opposites equalize one another, and gradually a new attitude develops, the final stability of which is the greater in proportion to the magnitude of the initial differences. The greater the tension between the pairs of opposites, the greater will be the energy that comes from them; and the greater the energy, the stronger will be its constellating, attracting power. This increased power of attraction corresponds to a wider range of constellated psychic material, and the further this range extends, the less chance is there of subsequent disturbances which might arise from friction with material not previously constellated. For this reason an attitude that has been formed out of a far-reaching process of equalization is an especially lasting one.

50   Daily psychological experience affords proof of this statement. The most intense conflicts, if overcome, leave behind a sense of security and calm which is not easily disturbed, or else a brokenness that can hardly be healed. Conversely, it is just these intense conflicts and their conflagration which are needed in order to produce valuable and lasting results. Since our experience is confined to relatively closed systems, we are never in a position to observe an absolute psychological entropy; but the more the psychological system is closed off, the more clearly is the phenomenon of entropy manifested.[43] We see this particularly well in those mental disturbances which are characterized by intense seclusion from the environment. The so-called "dulling of affect" in dementia praecox or schizophrenia may well be understood as a phenomenon of entropy. The same applies to all those so-called degenerative phenomena which develop in psychological attitudes that permanently ex-

42 *Populäre Schriften*, p. 33.
43 A system is absolutely closed when no energy from outside can be fed into it. Only in such a system can entropy occur.

clude all connection with the environment. Similarly, such voluntarily directed processes as directed thinking and directed feeling can be viewed as relatively closed psychological systems. These functions are based on the principle of the exclusion of the inappropriate, or unsuitable, which might bring about a deviation from the chosen path. The elements that "belong" are left to a process of mutual equalization, and meanwhile are protected from disturbing influences from outside. Thus after some time they reach their "probable" state, which shows its stability in, say, a "lasting" conviction or a "deeply ingrained" point of view, etc. How firmly such things are rooted can be tested by anyone who has attempted to dissolve such a structure, for instance to uproot a prejudice or change a habit of thought. In the history of nations these changes have cost rivers of blood. But in so far as absolute insulation is impossible (except, maybe, in pathological cases), the energic process continues as development, though, because of "loss by friction," with lessening intensity and decreased potential.

51   This way of looking at things has long been familiar. Everyone speaks of the "storms of youth" which yield to the "tranquillity of age." We speak, too, of a "confirmed belief" after "battling with doubts," of "relief from inner tension," and so on. This is the involuntary energic standpoint shared by everyone. For the scientific psychologist, of course, it remains valueless so long as he feels no need to estimate psychological values, while for physiological psychology this problem does not arise at all. Psychiatry, as opposed to psychology, is purely descriptive, and until recently it has not concerned itself at all about psychological causality, has in fact even denied it. Analytical psychology, however, was obliged to take the energic standpoint into account, since the causal-mechanistic standpoint of Freudian psychoanalysis was not sufficient to do justice to psychological values. Value requires for its explanation a quantitative concept, and a qualitative concept like sexuality can never serve as a substitute. A qualitative concept is always the description of a thing, a substance; whereas a quantitative concept deals with relations of intensity and never with a substance or a thing. A qualitative concept that does not designate a substance, a thing, or a fact is a more or less arbitrary exception, and as such I must count a qualitative, hypostatized concept of energy. A scientific

27

causal explanation now and then needs assumptions of this kind, yet they must not be taken over merely for the purpose of making an energic standpoint superfluous. The same is true of the theory of energy, which at times shows a tendency to deny substance in order to become purely teleological or finalistic. To substitute a qualitative concept for energy is inadmissible, for that would be a specification of energy, which is in fact a force. This would be in biology vitalism, in psychology sexualism (Freud), or some other "ism," in so far as it could be shown that the investigators reduced the energy of the total psyche to one definite force or drive. But drives, as we have shown, are specific forms of energy. Energy includes these in a higher concept of relation, and it cannot express anything else than the relations between psychological values.

d. Energism and Dynamism

52 What has been said above refers to a *pure* concept of energy. The concept of energy, like its correlate, the concept of time, is on the one hand an immediate, *a priori*, intuitive idea,[44] and on the other a concrete, applied, or empirical concept abstracted from experience, like all scientific explanatory concepts.[45] The *applied* concept of energy always deals with the behaviour of forces, with substances in motion; for energy is accessible to experience in no other way than through the observation of moving bodies. Hence, in practice, we speak of electrical energy and the like, as if energy were a definite force. This merging of

[44] Therefore the idea of it is as old as humanity. We meet it in the fundamental ideas of primitives. Cf. Lehmann, *Mana, der Begriff des 'ausserordentlich Wirkungsvollen' bei Südseevölkern,* and my remarks in *Two Essays on Analytical Psychology,* par. 108. Hubert and Mauss (*Mélanges d'histoire des religions,* preface, p. xxix) also call *mana* a "category" of the understanding. I quote their words verbatim: "[The categories] constantly manifested in language, though not necessarily explicit in it, exist as a rule rather in the form of habits that govern consciousness, while themselves unconscious. The notion of mana is one of these principles. It is a datum of language; it is implied in a whole series of judgements and reasonings concerned with attributes which are those of mana. We have called mana a category. But it is not only a category peculiar to primitive thought, and today, by reduction, it is still the first form taken on by other categories which are always operative in our minds, those of substance and cause," etc.

[45] [For a discussion of the formation of intuitive *vs.* empirical concepts, see *Psychological Types,* pars. 518ff., and Def. 22: "Function."]

the applied or empirical concept with the intuitive idea of the event gives rise to those constant confusions of "energy" with "force." Similarly, the psychological concept of energy is not a pure concept, but a concrete and applied concept that appears to us in the form of sexual, vital, mental, moral "energy," and so on. In other words, it appears in the form of a drive, the unmistakably dynamic nature of which justifies us in making a conceptual parallel with physical forces.

53   The application of the pure concept to the stuff of experience necessarily brings about a concretization or visualization of the concept, so that it looks as if a substance had been posited. This is the case, for instance, with the physicist's concept of ether, which, although a concept, is treated exactly as if it were a substance. This confusion is unavoidable, since we are incapable of imagining a quantum unless it be a quantum of something. This something is the substance. Therefore every applied concept is unavoidably hypostatized, even against our will, though we must never forget that what we are dealing with is still a concept.

54   I have suggested calling the energy concept used in analytical psychology by the name "libido." The choice of this term may not be ideal in some respects, yet it seemed to me that this concept merited the name libido if only for reasons of historical justice. Freud was the first to follow out these really dynamic, psychological relationships and to present them coherently, making use of the convenient term "libido," albeit with a specifically sexual connotation in keeping with his general starting-point, which was sexuality. Together with "libido" Freud used the expressions "drive" or "instinct" (e.g., "ego-instincts") [46] and "psychic energy." Since Freud confines himself almost exclusively to sexuality and its manifold ramifications in the psyche, the sexual definition of energy as a specific driving force is quite sufficient for his purpose. In a general psychological theory, however, it is impossible to use purely sexual energy, that is, one specific drive, as an explanatory concept, since psychic energy transformation is not merely a matter of sexual

---

[46] [Jung here uses the terms *Trieb* and *Ichtriebe* (lit. "drive," "ego-drives") following Freud's German terminology. Freud's terms have been trans. into English as "instinct" and "ego-instincts." Cf., e.g., Freud, *Introductory Lectures*, pp. 294ff.—EDITORS.]

dynamics. Sexual dynamics is only one particular instance in the total field of the psyche. This is not to deny its existence, but merely to put it in its proper place.

55   Since, for our concretistic thinking, the applied concept of energy immediately hypostatizes itself as the psychic forces (drives, affects, and other dynamic processes), its concrete character is in my view aptly expressed by the term "libido." Similar conceptions have always made use of designations of this kind, for instance Schopenhauer's "Will," Aristotle's ὁρμή, Plato's Eros, Empedocles' "love and hate of the elements," or the *élan vital* of Bergson. From these concepts I have borrowed only the concrete character of the term, not the definition of the concept. The omission of a detailed explanation of this in my earlier book is responsible for numerous misunderstandings, such as the accusation that I have built up a kind of vitalistic concept.

56   While I do not connect any specifically sexual definition with the word "libido," [47] this is not to deny the existence of a sexual dynamism any more than any other dynamism, for instance that of the hunger-drive, etc. As early as 1912 I pointed out that my conception of a general life instinct, named libido, takes the place of the concept of "psychic energy" which I used in "The Psychology of Dementia Praecox." I was, however, guilty of a sin of omission in presenting the concept only in its psychological concreteness and leaving out of account its metaphysical aspect, which is the subject of the present discussion. But, by leaving the libido concept wholly in its concrete form, I treated it as though it were hypostatized. Thus far I am to blame for the misunderstandings. I therefore expressly declared, in my "Theory of Psychoanalysis," [48] published in 1913, that "the libido with which we operate is not only not concrete or known, but is a complete X, a pure hypothesis, a model or counter, and is no more concretely conceivable than the energy known to the world of physics." Libido, therefore, is nothing but an abbreviated expression for the "energic standpoint." In a concrete presentation we shall never be able to operate with pure concepts unless we succeed in expressing the phenomenon mathe-

[47] The Latin word *libido* has by no means an exclusively sexual connotation, but the general meaning of desire, longing, urge. Cf. *Symbols of Transformation*, pars. 185ff.   [48] *Freud and Psychoanalysis*, par. 282.

matically. So long as this is impossible, the applied concept will automatically become hypostatized through the data of experience.

57 We must note yet another obscurity arising out of the concrete use of the libido-concept and of the concept of energy in general, namely the confusion, unavoidable in practical experience, of energy with the causal concept of effect, which is a dynamic and not an energic concept at all.

58 The causal-mechanistic view sees the sequence of facts, a-b-c-d, as follows: a causes b, b causes c, and so on. Here the concept of effect appears as the designation of a quality, as a "virtue" of the cause, in other words, as a dynamism. The final-energic view, on the other hand, sees the sequence thus: a-b-c are means towards the transformation of energy, which flows causelessly from a, the improbable state, entropically to b-c and so to the probable state d. Here a causal effect is totally disregarded, since only intensities of effect are taken into account. In so far as the intensities are the same, we could just as well put w-x-y-z instead of a-b-c-d.

59 The datum of experience is in both cases the sequence a-b-c-d, with the difference that the mechanistic view infers a dynamism from the causal effect observed, while the energic view observes the equivalence of the transformed effect rather than the effect of a cause. That is to say, both observe the sequence a-b-c-d, the one qualitatively, the other quantitatively. The causal mode of thought abstracts the dynamic concept from the datum of experience, while the final view applies its pure concept of energy to the field of observation and allows it, as it were, to become a dynamism. Despite their epistemological differences, which are as absolute as could be wished, the two modes of observation are unavoidably blended in the concept of force, the causal view abstracting its pure perception of the operative quality into a concept of dynamism, and the final view allowing its pure concept to become concretized through application. Thus the mechanist speaks of the "energy of *the psychic*," while the energist speaks of "psychic *energy*." From what has been said it should be evident that one and the same process takes on different aspects according to the different standpoints from which it is viewed.

III. FUNDAMENTAL CONCEPTS OF THE LIBIDO THEORY

a. *Progression and Regression*

60   One of the most important energic phenomena of psychic life is the progression and regression of libido. Progression could be defined as the daily advance of the process of psychological adaptation. We know that adaptation is not something that is achieved once and for all, though there is a tendency to believe the contrary. This is due to mistaking a person's psychic attitude for actual adaptation. We can satisfy the demands of adaptation only by means of a suitably directed attitude. Consequently, the achievement of adaptation is completed in two stages: (1) attainment of attitude, (2) completion of adaptation by means of the attitude. A man's attitude to reality is something extraordinarily persistent, but the more persistent his mental habitus is, the less permanent will be his effective achievement of adaptation. This is the necessary consequence of the continual changes in the environment and the new adaptations demanded by them.

61   The progression of libido might therefore be said to consist in a continual satisfaction of the demands of environmental conditions. This is possible only by means of an attitude, which as such is necessarily directed and therefore characterized by a certain one-sidedness. Thus it may easily happen that an attitude can no longer satisfy the demands of adaptation because changes have occurred in the environmental conditions which require a different attitude. For example, a feeling-attitude that seeks to fulfil the demands of reality by means of empathy may easily encounter a situation that can only be solved through thinking. In this case the feeling-attitude breaks down and the progression of libido also ceases. The vital feeling that was present before disappears, and in its place the psychic value of certain conscious contents increases in an unpleasant way; subjective contents and reactions press to the fore and the situation becomes full of affect and ripe for explosions. These symptoms indicate a damming up of libido, and the stoppage is always marked by the breaking up of the pairs of opposites. During the progression of libido the pairs of opposites are united in the co-ordinated flow of psychic processes. Their working together makes possible the

balanced regularity of these processes, which without this inner polarity would become one-sided and unreasonable. We are therefore justified in regarding all extravagant and exaggerated behaviour as a loss of balance, because the co-ordinating effect of the opposite impulse is obviously lacking. Hence it is essential for progression, which is the successful achievement of adaptation, that impulse and counter-impulse, positive and negative, should reach a state of regular interaction and mutual influence. This balancing and combining of pairs of opposites can be seen, for instance, in the process of reflection that precedes a difficult decision. But in the stoppage of libido that occurs when progression has become impossible, positive and negative can no longer unite in co-ordinated action, because both have attained an equal value which keeps the scales balanced. The longer the stoppage lasts, the more the value of the opposed positions increases; they become enriched with more and more associations and attach to themselves an ever-widening range of psychic material. The tension leads to conflict, the conflict leads to attempts at mutual repression, and if one of the opposing forces is successfully repressed a dissociation ensues, a splitting of the personality, or disunion with oneself. The stage is then set for a neurosis. The acts that follow from such a condition are unco-ordinated, sometimes pathological, having the appearance of symptomatic actions. Although in part normal, they are based partly on the repressed opposite which, instead of working as an equilibrating force, has an obstructive effect, thus hindering the possibility of further progress.

62   The struggle between the opposites would persist in this fruitless way if the process of regression, the backward movement of libido, did not set in with the outbreak of the conflict. Through their collision the opposites are gradually deprived of value and depotentiated. This loss of value steadily increases and is the only thing perceived by consciousness. It is synonymous with regression, for in proportion to the decrease in value of the conscious opposites there is an increase in the value of all those psychic processes which are not concerned with outward adaptation and therefore are seldom or never employed consciously. These psychic factors are for the most part unconscious. As the value of the subliminal elements and of the unconscious increases, it is to be expected that they will gain influence over

the conscious mind. On account of the inhibiting influence which the conscious exercises over the unconscious, the unconscious values assert themselves at first only indirectly. The inhibition to which they are subjected is a result of the exclusive directedness of conscious contents. (This inhibition is identical with what Freud calls the "censor.") The indirect manifestation of the unconscious takes the form of disturbances of conscious behaviour. In the association experiment they appear as complex-indicators, in daily life as the "symptomatic actions" first described by Freud, and in neurotic conditions they appear as symptoms.

63   Since regression raises the value of contents that were previously excluded from the conscious process of adaptation, and hence are either totally unconscious or only "dimly conscious," the psychic elements now being forced over the threshold are momentarily useless from the standpoint of adaptation, and for this reason are invariably kept at a distance by the directed psychic function. The nature of these contents is for all the world to read in Freudian literature. They are not only of an infantile-sexual character, but are altogether incompatible contents and tendencies, partly immoral, partly unaesthetic, partly again of an irrational, imaginary nature. The obviously inferior character of these contents as regards adaptation has given rise to that depreciatory view of the psychic background which is habitual in psychoanalytic writings.[49] What the regression brings to the surface certainly seems at first sight to be slime from the depths; but if one does not stop short at a superficial evaluation and refrains from passing judgment on the basis of a preconceived dogma, it will be found that this "slime" contains not merely incompatible and rejected remnants of every-

---

[49] Somewhat after the manner of Hudibras, whose opinion is quoted by Kant (*Träume eines Geistersehers*, III): "When a hypochondriacal wind is roaring in the bowels, everything depends on the direction it takes. If it goes downwards, it turns into a fart, but if it mounts upwards, it is a vision or a divine inspiration." [For a much bowdlerized version see *Dreams of a Spirit-Seer*, trans. by Emanuel Goerwitz, p. 84. Kant's version is presumably based on Samuel Butler's *Hudibras*, Part II, Canto iii, lines 773-76:

> "As wind i' th' *Hypochondrias* pent
> Is but a blast if downward sent;
> But if it upwards chance to fly
> Becomes new *Light* and *Prophecy*."—TRANS.]

day life, or inconvenient and objectionable animal tendencies, but also germs of new life and vital possibilities for the future.[50] This is one of the great merits of psychoanalysis, that it is not afraid to dredge up the incompatible elements, which would be a thoroughly useless and indeed reprehensible undertaking were it not for the possibilities of new life that lie in the repressed contents. That this is and must be so is not only proved by a wealth of practical experience but can also be deduced from the following considerations.

64   The process of adaptation requires a directed conscious function characterized by inner consistency and logical coherence. Because it is directed, everything unsuitable must be excluded in order to maintain the integrity of direction. The unsuitable elements are subjected to inhibition and thereby escape attention. Now experience shows that there is only *one* consciously directed function of adaptation. If, for example, I have a thinking orientation I cannot at the same time orient myself by feeling, because thinking and feeling are two quite different functions. In fact, I must carefully exclude feeling if I am to satisfy the logical laws of thinking, so that the thought-process will not be disturbed by feeling. In this case I withdraw as much libido as possible from the feeling process, with the result that this function becomes relatively unconscious. Experience shows, again, that the orientation is largely habitual; accordingly the other unsuitable functions, so far as they are incompatible with the prevailing attitude, are relatively unconscious, and hence unused, untrained, and undifferentiated. Moreover, on the principle of coexistence they necessarily become associated with other contents of the unconscious, the inferior and incompatible quality of which I have already pointed out. Consequently, when these functions are activated by regression and so reach consciousness, they appear in a somewhat incompatible form, disguised and covered up with the slime of the deep.

65   If we remember that the stoppage of libido was due to the failure of the conscious attitude, we can now understand what valuable seeds lie in the unconscious contents activated by regression. They contain the elements of that other function

50 Though professional satiety with neurotic unrealities makes the analyst sceptical, a generalized judgment from the pathological angle has the disadvantage of being always biased.

which was excluded by the conscious attitude and which would be capable of effectively complementing or even of replacing the inadequate conscious attitude. If thinking fails as the adapted function, because it is dealing with a situation to which one can adapt only by feeling, then the unconscious material activated by regression will contain the missing feeling function, although still in embryonic form, archaic and undeveloped. Similarly, in the opposite type, regression would activate a thinking function that would effectively compensate the inadequate feeling.

66   By activating an unconscious factor, regression confronts consciousness with the problem of the psyche as opposed to the problem of outward adaptation. It is natural that the conscious mind should fight against accepting the regressive contents, yet it is finally compelled by the impossibility of further progress to submit to the regressive values. In other words, regression leads to the necessity of adapting to the inner world of the psyche.

67   Just as adaptation to the environment may fail because of the one-sidedness of the adapted function, so adaptation to the inner world may fail because of the one-sidedness of the function in question. For instance, if the stoppage of libido was due to the failure of the thinking attitude to cope with the demands of outward adaptation, and if the unconscious feeling function is activated by regression, there is only a feeling attitude towards the inner world. This may be sufficient at first, but in the long run it will cease to be adequate, and the thinking function will have to be enlisted too, just as the reverse was necessary when dealing with the outer world. Thus a complete orientation towards the inner world becomes necessary until such time as inner adaptation is attained. Once the adaptation is achieved, progression can begin again.

68   The principle of progression and regression is portrayed in the myth of the whale-dragon worked out by Frobenius,[51] as I have shown in detail in my book *Symbols of Transformation* (pars. 307ff.). The hero is the symbolical exponent of the movement of libido. Entry into the dragon is the regressive direction, and the journey to the East (the "night sea journey") with its attendant events symbolizes the effort to adapt to the conditions

---

[51] *Das Zeitalter des Sonnengottes.*

of the psychic inner world. The complete swallowing up and disappearance of the hero in the belly of the dragon represents the complete withdrawal of interest from the outer world. The overcoming of the monster from within is the achievement of adaptation to the conditions of the inner world, and the emergence ("slipping out") of the hero from the monster's belly with the help of a bird, which happens at the moment of sunrise, symbolizes the recommencement of progression.

69 It is characteristic that the monster begins the night sea journey to the East, i.e., towards sunrise, while the hero is engulfed in its belly. This seems to me to indicate that regression is not necessarily a retrograde step in the sense of a backwards development or degeneration, but rather represents a necessary phase of development. The individual is, however, not consciously aware that he is developing; he feels himself to be in a compulsive situation that resembles an early infantile state or even an embryonic condition within the womb. It is only if he remains stuck in this condition that we can speak of involution or degeneration.

70 Again, *progression* should not be confused with *development*, for the continuous flow or current of life is not necessarily development and differentiation. From primeval times certain plant and animal species have remained at a standstill without further differentiation, and yet have continued in existence. In the same way the psychic life of man can be progressive without evolution and regressive without involution. Evolution and involution have as a matter of fact no immediate connection with progression and regression, since the latter are mere life-movements which, notwithstanding their direction, actually have a static character. They correspond to what Goethe has aptly described as systole and diastole.[52]

71 Many objections have been raised against the view that myths represent psychological facts. People are very loath to

[52] Diastole is an extraversion of libido spreading through the entire universe; systole is its contraction into the individual, the monad. ("Systole, the conscious, powerful contraction that brings forth the individual, and diastole, the longing to embrace the All." Chamberlain, *Goethe,* p. 571.) To remain in either of these attitudes means death (p. 571), hence the one type is insufficient and needs complementing by the opposite function. ("If a man holds himself exclusively in the receptive attitude, if diastole persists indefinitely, then there enters into his psychic life, as into his bodily life, crippling and finally death. Only action can

give up the idea that the myth is some kind of explanatory allegory of astronomical, meteorological, or vegetative processes. The coexistence of explanatory tendencies is certainly not to be denied, since there is abundant proof that myths also have an explanatory significance, but we are still faced with the question: why should myths explain things in this allegorical way? It is essential to understand where the primitive gets this explanatory material from, for it should not be forgotten that the primitive's need of causal explanations is not nearly so great as it is with us. He is far less interested in explaining things than in weaving fables. We can see almost daily in our patients how mythical fantasies arise: they are not thought up, but present themselves as images or chains of ideas that force their way out of the unconscious, and when they are recounted they often have the character of connected episodes resembling mythical dramas. That is how myths arise, and that is the reason why the fantasies from the unconscious have so much in common with primitive myths. But in so far as the myth is nothing but a projection from the unconscious and not a conscious invention at all, it is quite understandable that we should everywhere come upon the same myth-motifs, and that myths actually represent typical psychic phenomena.

72   We must now consider how the processes of progression and regression are to be understood energically. That they are essentially dynamic processes should by now be sufficiently clear. Progression might be compared to a watercourse that flows from a mountain into a valley. The damming up of libido is analogous to a specific obstruction in the direction of the flow, such as a dike, which transforms the kinetic energy of the flow into the potential energy of a reservoir. Thus dammed back, the water is forced into another channel, if as a result of the damming it reaches a level that permits it to flow off in another direction. Perhaps it will flow into a channel where the energy arising from the difference in potential is transformed into electricity by means of a turbine. This transformation might serve as a model for the new progression brought about by the dam-

animate, and its first condition is limitation, i.e., systole, which creates a firmly bounded measure. The more energetic the act, the more resolute must be the enforcing of the limitation."—p. 581.)

ming up and regression, its changed character being indicated by the new way in which the energy now manifests itself. In this process of transformation the principle of equivalence has a special heuristic value: the intensity of progression reappears in the intensity of regression.

73   It is not an essential postulate of the energic standpoint that there must be progression and regression of libido, only that there must be equivalent transformations, for energetics is concerned only with quantity and makes no attempt to explain quality. Thus progression and regression are specific processes which must be conceived as dynamic, and which as such are conditioned by the qualities of matter. They cannot in any sense be derived from the essential nature of the concept of energy, though in their reciprocal relations they can only be understood energically. Why progression and regression should exist at all can only be explained by the qualities of matter, that is by means of a mechanistic-causal hypothesis.

74   Progression as a continuous process of adaptation to environmental conditions springs from the vital need for such adaptation. Necessity enforces complete orientation to these conditions and the suppression of all those tendencies and possibilities which subserve individuation.

75   Regression, on the other hand, as an adaptation to the conditions of the inner world, springs from the vital need to satisfy the demands of individuation. Man is not a machine in the sense that he can consistently maintain the same output of work. He can meet the demands of outer necessity in an ideal way only if he is also adapted to his own inner world, that is, if he is in harmony with himself. Conversely, he can only adapt to his inner world and achieve harmony with himself when he is adapted to the environmental conditions. As experience shows, the one or the other function can be neglected only for a time. If, for example, there is only one-sided adaptation to the outer world while the inner one is neglected, the value of the inner world will gradually increase, and this shows itself in the irruption of personal elements into the sphere of outer adaptation. I once saw a drastic instance of this: A manufacturer who had worked his way up to a high level of success and prosperity began to remember a certain phase of his youth when he took great pleasure in art. He felt the need to return to these pursuits,

and began making artistic designs for the wares he manufactured. The result was that nobody wanted to buy these artistic products, and the man became bankrupt after a few years. His mistake lay in carrying over into the outer world what belonged to the inner, because he misunderstood the demands of individuation. So striking a failure of a function that was adequately adapted before can only be explained by this typical misunderstanding of the inner demands.

76   Although progression and regression are causally grounded in the nature of the life-processes on the one hand and in environmental conditions on the other, yet, if we look at them energically, we must think of them only as a means, as transitional stages in the flow of energy. Looked at from this angle, progression and the adaptation resulting therefrom are a means to regression, to a manifestation of the inner world in the outer. In this way a new means is created for a changed mode of progression, bringing better adaptation to environmental conditions.

b. *Extraversion and Introversion*

77   Progression and regression can be brought into relationship with extraversion and introversion: progression, as adaptation to outer conditions, could be regarded as extraversion; regression, as adaptation to inner conditions, could be regarded as introversion. But this parallel would give rise to a great deal of conceptual confusion, since progression and regression are at best only vague analogies of extraversion and introversion. In reality the latter two concepts represent dynamisms of a different kind from progression and regression. These are dynamic forms of a specifically determined transformation of energy, whereas extraversion and introversion, as their names suggest, are the forms taken both by progression and by regression. Progression is a forwards movement of life in the same sense that time moves forwards. This movement can occur in two different forms: either extraverted, when the progression is predominantly influenced by objects and environmental conditions, or introverted, when it has to adapt itself to the conditions of the ego (or, more accurately, of the "subjective factor"). Similarly, regression can proceed along two lines: either as a retreat from

the outside world (introversion), or as a flight into extravagant experience of the outside world (extraversion). Failure in the first case drives a man into a state of dull brooding, and in the second case into leading the life of a wastrel. These two different ways of reacting, which I have called introversion and extraversion, correspond to two opposite types of attitude and are described in detail in my book *Psychological Types*.

78 Libido moves not only forwards and backwards, but also outwards and inwards. The psychology of the latter movement is described at some length in my book on types, so I can refrain from further elaboration here.

c. The Canalization of Libido

79 In my *Symbols of Transformation* (pars. 203f.) I used the expression "canalization of libido" to characterize the process of energic transformation or conversion. I mean by this a transfer of psychic intensities or values from one content to another, a process corresponding to the physical transformation of energy; for example, in the steam-engine the conversion of heat into the pressure of steam and then into the energy of motion. Similarly, the energy of certain psychological phenomena is converted by suitable means into other dynamisms. In the above-mentioned book I have given examples of these transformation processes and need not elaborate them here.

80 When Nature is left to herself, energy is transformed along the line of its natural "gradient." In this way natural phenomena are produced, but not "work." So also man when left to himself lives as a natural phenomenon, and, in the proper meaning of the word, produces no work. It is culture that provides the machine whereby the natural gradient is exploited for the performance of work. That man should ever have invented this machine must be due to something rooted deep in his nature, indeed in the nature of the living organism as such. For living matter is itself a transformer of energy, and in some way as yet unknown life participates in the transformation process. Life proceeds, as it were, by making use of natural physical and chemical conditions as a means to its own existence. The living body is a machine for converting the energies it uses into other dynamic manifestations that are their

equivalents. We cannot say that physical energy is transformed into life, only that its transformation is the expression of life.

81   In the same way that the living body as a whole is a machine, other adaptations to physical and chemical conditions have the value of machines that make other forms of transformation possible. Thus all the means an animal employs for safeguarding and furthering its existence—apart from the direct nourishment of its body—can be regarded as machines that exploit the natural gradient for the performance of work. When the beaver fells trees and dams up a river, this is a performance conditioned by its differentiation. Its differentiation is a product of what one might call "natural culture," which functions as a transformer of energy, as a machine. Similarly human culture, as a natural product of differentiation, is a machine; first of all a technical one that utilizes natural conditions for the transformation of physical and chemical energy, but also a psychic machine that utilizes psychic conditions for the transformation of libido.

82   Just as man has succeeded in inventing a turbine, and, by conducting a flow of water to it, in transforming the latter's kinetic energy into electricity capable of manifold applications, so he has succeeded, with the help of a psychic mechanism, in converting natural instincts, which would otherwise follow their gradient without performing work, into other dynamic forms that are productive of work.

83   The transformation of instinctual energy is achieved by its canalization into an *analogue of the object of instinct.* Just as a power-station imitates a waterfall and thereby gains possession of its energy, so the psychic mechanism imitates the instinct and is thereby enabled to apply its energy for special purposes. A good example of this is the spring ceremony performed by the Wachandi, of Australia.[53] They dig a hole in the ground, oval in shape and set about with bushes so that it looks like a woman's genitals. Then they dance round this hole, holding their spears in front of them in imitation of an erect penis. As they dance round, they thrust their spears into the hole, shouting: "Pulli nira, pulli nira, wataka!" (not a pit, not a pit, but a c——!). During the ceremony none of the participants is allowed to look at a woman.

[53] Preuss, "Der Ursprung der Religion und Kunst," p. 388; Schultze, *Psychologie der Naturvölker,* p. 168; *Symbols of Transformation,* pars. 213f.

84 By means of the hole the Wachandi make an analogue of the female genitals, the object of natural instinct. By the reiterated shouting and the ecstasy of the dance they suggest to themselves that the hole is really a vulva, and in order not to have this illusion disturbed by the real object of instinct, none may look at a woman. There can be no doubt that this is a canalization of energy and its transference to an analogue of the original object by means of the dance (which is really a mating-play, as with birds and other animals) and by imitating the sexual act.[54]

85 This dance has a special significance as an earth-impregnation ceremony and therefore takes place in the spring. It is a magical act for the purpose of transferring libido to the earth, whereby the earth acquires a special psychic value and becomes an object of expectation. The mind then busies itself with the earth, and in turn is affected by it, so that there is a possibility and even a probability that man will give it his attention, which is the psychological prerequisite for cultivation. Agriculture did in fact arise, though not exclusively, from the formation of sexual analogies. The "bridal bed in the field" is a canalization ceremony of this kind: on a spring night the farmer takes his wife into the field and has intercourse with her there, in order to make the earth fruitful. In this way a very close analogy is established, which acts like a channel that conducts water from a river to a power-station. The instinctual energy becomes closely associated with the field, so that the cultivation of it acquires the value of a sexual act. This association assures a permanent flow of interest to the field, which accordingly exerts an attraction on the cultivator. He is thus induced to occupy himself with the field in a way that is obviously beneficial to fertility.

86 As Meringer has convincingly shown, the association of libido (also in the sexual sense) and agriculture is expressed in linguistic usage.[55] The putting of libido into the earth is achieved not by sexual analogy alone, but by the "magic touch," as in the custom of rolling (wälzen, walen) in the field.[56]

---

54 Cf. the observation in Pechuël-Loesche, Volkskunde von Loango, p. 38: the dancers scrape the ground with one foot and at the same time carry out specific abdominal movements.

55 "Wörter und Sachen." Cf. Symbols of Transformation, par. 214, n. 21.

56 Mannhardt, Wald- und Feldkulte, I, pp. 48off.

To primitive man the canalization of libido is so concrete a thing that he even feels fatigue from work as a state of being "sucked dry" by the daemon of the field.[57] All major undertakings and efforts, such as tilling the soil, hunting, war, etc., are entered upon with ceremonies of magical analogy or with preparatory incantations which quite obviously have the psychological aim of canalizing libido into the necessary activity. In the buffalo-dances of the Taos Pueblo Indians the dancers represent both the hunters and the game. Through the excitement and pleasure of the dance the libido is channelled into the form of hunting activity. The pleasure required for this is produced by rhythmic drumming and the stirring chants of the old men who direct the whole ceremony. It is well known that old people live in their memories and love to speak of their former deeds; this "warms" them. Warmth "kindles," and thus the old men in a sense give the first impulse to the dance, to the mimetic ceremony whose aim is to accustom the young men and boys to the hunt and to prepare them for it psychologically. Similar *rites d'entrée* are reported of many primitive tribes.[58] A classic example of this is the *atninga* ceremony of the Aruntas, of Australia. It consists in first stirring to anger the members of a tribe who are summoned for an expedition of revenge. This is done by the leader tying the hair of the dead man to be avenged to the mouth and penis of the man who is to be made angry. Then the leader kneels on the man and embraces him as if performing the sexual act with him.[59] It is supposed that in this way "the bowels of the man will begin to burn with desire to avenge the murder." The point of the ceremony is obviously to bring about an intimate acquaintance of each individual with the murdered man, so that each is made ready to avenge the dead.

87   The enormous complexity of such ceremonies shows how much is needed to divert the libido from its natural river-bed of everyday habit into some unaccustomed activity. The modern mind thinks this can be done by a mere decision of the will and

[57] Ibid., p. 483.

[58] A comprehensive survey in Lévy-Bruhl, *How Natives Think*, trans. by Clare, pp. 228ff.

[59] See illustration in Spencer and Gillen, *The Northern Tribes of Central Australia,* p. 560.

that it can dispense with all magical ceremonies—which explains why it was so long at a loss to understand them properly. But when we remember that primitive man is much more unconscious, much more of a "natural phenomenon" than we are, and has next to no knowledge of what we call "will," then it is easy to understand why he needs complicated ceremonies where a simple act of will is sufficient for us. We are more conscious, that is to say more domesticated. In the course of the millennia we have succeeded not only in conquering the wild nature all round us, but in subduing our own wildness—at least temporarily and up to a point. At all events we have been acquiring "will," i.e., disposable energy, and though it may not amount to much it is nevertheless more than the primitive possesses. We no longer need magical dances to make us "strong" for whatever we want to do, at least not in ordinary cases. But when we have to do something that exceeds our powers, something that might easily go wrong, then we solemnly lay a foundation-stone with the blessing of the Church, or we "christen" a ship as she slips from the docks; in time of war we assure ourselves of the help of a patriotic God, the sweat of fear forcing a fervent prayer from the lips of the stoutest. So it only needs slightly insecure conditions for the "magical" formalities to be resuscitated in the most natural way. Through these ceremonies the deeper emotional forces are released; conviction becomes blind auto-suggestion, and the psychic field of vision is narrowed to one fixed point on which the whole weight of the unconscious forces is concentrated. And it is, indeed, an objective fact that success attends the sure rather than the unsure.

d. Symbol Formation

88   The psychological mechanism that transforms energy is the symbol. I mean by this a real symbol and not a sign. The Wachandi's hole in the earth is not a sign for the genitals of a woman, but a symbol that stands for the idea of the earth woman who is to be made fruitful. To mistake it for a human woman would be to interpret the symbol semiotically, and this would fatally disturb the value of the ceremony. It is for this reason that none of the dancers may look at a woman. The mechanism would be destroyed by a semiotic interpretation—it would be like

45

smashing the supply-pipe of a turbine on the ground that it was a very unnatural waterfall that owed its existence to the repression of natural conditions. I am far from suggesting that the semiotic interpretation is meaningless; it is not only a possible interpretation but also a very true one. Its usefulness is undisputed in all those cases where nature is merely thwarted without any effective work resulting from it. But the semiotic interpretation becomes meaningless when it is applied exclusively and schematically—when, in short, it ignores the real nature of the symbol and debases it to a mere sign.

89   The first achievement wrested by primitive man from instinctual energy, through analogy-building, is magic. A ceremony is magical so long as it does not result in effective work but preserves the state of expectancy. In that case the energy is canalized into a new object and produces a new dynamism, which in turn remains magical so long as it does not create effective work. The advantage accruing from a magical ceremony is that the newly invested object acquires a working potential in relation to the psyche. Because of its value it has a determining and stimulating effect on the imagination, so that for a long time the mind is fascinated and possessed by it. This gives rise to actions that are performed in a half-playful way on the magical object, most of them rhythmical in character. A good example is those South American rock-drawings which consist of furrows deeply engraved in the hard stone. They were made by the Indians playfully retracing the furrows again and again with stones, over hundreds of years. The content of the drawings is difficult to interpret, but the activity bound up with them is incomparably more significant.[60]

90   The influence exerted on the mind by the magically effective object has other possible consequences. Through a sustained playful interest in the object, a man may make all sorts of discoveries about it which would otherwise have escaped him. As we know, many discoveries have actually been made in this way. Not for nothing is magic called the "mother of science." Until late in the Middle Ages what we today call science was nothing other than magic. A striking example of this is alchemy, whose symbolism shows quite unmistakably the principle of

[60] Koch-Grünberg, *Südamerikanische Felszeichnungen.*

transformation of energy described above, and indeed the later alchemists were fully conscious of this fact.[61] But only through the development of magic into science, that is, through the advance from the stage of mere expectation to real technical work on the object, have we acquired that mastery over the forces of nature of which the age of magic dreamed. Even the alchemist's dream of the transmutation of the elements has been fulfilled, and magical action at a distance has been realized by the discovery of electricity. So we have every reason to value symbol-formation and to render homage to the symbol as an inestimable means of utilizing the mere instinctual flow of energy for effective work. A waterfall is certainly more beautiful than a power-station, but dire necessity teaches us to value electric light and electrified industry more highly than the superb wastefulness of a waterfall that delights us for a quarter of an hour on a holiday walk.

91   Just as in physical nature only a very small portion of natural energy can be converted into a usable form, and by far the greater part must be left to work itself out unused in natural phenomena, so in our psychic nature only a small part of the total energy can be diverted from its natural flow. An incomparably greater part cannot be utilized by us, but goes to sustain the regular course of life. Hence the libido is apportioned by nature to the various functional systems, from which it cannot be wholly withdrawn. The libido is invested in these functions as a specific force that cannot be transformed. Only where a symbol offers a steeper gradient than nature is it possible to canalize libido into other forms. The history of civilization has amply demonstrated that man possesses a relative surplus of energy that is capable of application apart from the natural flow. The fact that the symbol makes this deflection possible proves that not all the libido is bound up in a form that enforces the natural flow, but that a certain amount of energy remains over, which could be called excess libido. It is conceivable that this excess may be due to failure of the firmly organized functions to equalize differences in intensity. They might be compared to a system of water-pipes whose diameter is too small to draw off the water that is being steadily supplied. The water would then

61 Silberer, *Problems of Mysticism and Its Symbolism;* also Rosencreutz, *Chymische Hochzeit* (1616).

have to flow off in one way or another. From this excess libido certain psychic processes arise which cannot be explained—or only very inadequately—as the result of merely natural conditions. How are we to explain religious processes, for instance, whose nature is essentially symbolical? In abstract form, symbols are religious ideas; in the form of action, they are rites or ceremonies. They are the manifestation and expression of excess libido. At the same time they are stepping-stones to new activities, which must be called cultural in order to distinguish them from the instinctual functions that run their regular course according to natural law.

92   I have called a symbol that converts energy a "libido analogue." [62] By this I mean an idea that can give equivalent expression to the libido and canalize it into a form different from the original one. Mythology offers numerous equivalents of this kind, ranging from sacred objects such as *churingas,* fetishes, etc., to the figures of gods. The rites with which the sacred objects are surrounded often reveal very clearly their nature as transformers of energy. Thus the primitive rubs his *churinga* rhythmically and takes the magic power of the fetish into himself, at the same time giving it a fresh "charge." [63] A higher stage of the same line of thought is the idea of the totem, which is closely bound up with the beginnings of tribal life and leads straight to the idea of the palladium, the tutelary tribal deity, and to the idea of an organized human community in general. The transformation of libido through the symbol is a process that has been going on ever since the beginnings of humanity and continues still. Symbols were never devised consciously, but were always produced out of the unconscious by way of revelation or intuition.[64] In view of the close connection between mythological symbols and dream-symbols, and of the fact that the dream is "le dieu des sauvages," it is more than probable that most of the historical symbols derive directly from dreams

---

[62] *Symbols of Transformation,* pars. 146, 203.   [63] Spencer and Gillen, p. 277.
[64] "Man, of course, has always been trying to understand and to control his environment, but in the early stages this process was unconscious. The matters which are problems for us existed latent in the primitive brain; there, undefined, lay both problem and answer; through many ages of savagery, first one and then another partial answer emerged into consciousness; at the end of the series, hardly completed today, there will be a new synthesis in which riddle and answer are one." Crawley, *The Idea of the Soul,* p. 11.

or are at least influenced by them.[65] We know that this is true of the choice of totem, and there is similar evidence regarding the choice of gods. This age-old function of the symbol is still present today, despite the fact that for many centuries the trend of mental development has been towards the suppression of individual symbol-formation. One of the first steps in this direction was the setting up of an official state religion, a further step was the extermination of polytheism, first attempted in the reforms of Amenophis IV. We know the extraordinary part played by Christianity in the suppression of individual symbol-formation. But as the intensity of the Christian idea begins to fade, a recrudescence of individual symbol-formation may be expected. The prodigious increase of Christian sects since the eighteenth century, the century of "enlightenment," bears eloquent witness to this. Christian Science, theosophy, anthroposophy, and "Mazdaznan" are further steps along the same path.

93   In practical work with our patients we come upon symbol-formations at every turn, the purpose of which is the transformation of libido. At the beginning of treatment we find the symbol-forming process at work, but in an unsuitable form that offers the libido too low a gradient. Instead of being converted into effective work, the libido flows off unconsciously along the old channels, that is, into archaic sexual fantasies and fantasy activities. Accordingly the patient remains at war with himself, in other words, neurotic. In such cases analysis in the strict sense is indicated, i.e., the reductive psychoanalytic method inaugurated by Freud, which breaks down all inappropriate symbol-formations and reduces them to their natural elements. The power-station, situated too high and unsuitably constructed, is dismantled and separated into its original components, so that the natural flow is restored. The unconscious continues to produce symbols which one could obviously go on reducing to their elements *ad infinitum*.

94   But man can never rest content with the natural course of things, because he always has an excess of libido that can be offered a more favourable gradient than the merely natural one. For this reason he will inevitably seek it, no matter how often

[65] "Dreams are to the savage man what the Bible is to us—the source of divine revelation." Gatschet, "The Klamath Indians of South-Western Oregon," cited in Lévy-Bruhl, p. 57.

he may be forced back by reduction to the natural gradient. We have therefore reached the conclusion that when the unsuitable structures have been reduced and the natural course of things is restored, so that there is some possibility of the patient living a normal life, the reductive process should not be continued further. Instead, symbol-formation should be reinforced in a synthetic direction until a more favourable gradient for the excess libido is found. Reduction to the natural condition is neither an ideal state nor a panacea. If the natural state were really the ideal one, then the primitive would be leading an enviable existence. But that is by no means so, for aside from all the other sorrows and hardships of human life the primitive is tormented by superstitions, fears, and compulsions to such a degree that, if he lived in our civilization, he could not be described as other than profoundly neurotic, if not mad. What would one say of a European who conducted himself as follows? —A Negro dreamt that he was pursued by his enemies, caught, and burned alive. The next day he got his relatives to make a fire and told them to hold his feet in it, in order, by this apotropaic ceremony, to avert the misfortune of which he had dreamed. He was so badly burned that for many months he was unable to walk.[66]

95   Mankind was freed from these fears by a continual process of symbol-formation that leads to culture. Reversion to nature must therefore be followed by a synthetic reconstruction of the symbol. Reduction leads down to the primitive natural man and his peculiar mentality. Freud directed his attention mainly to the ruthless desire for pleasure, Adler to the "psychology of prestige." These are certainly two quite essential peculiarities of the primitive psyche, but they are far from being the only ones. For the sake of completeness we would have to mention other characteristics of the primitive, such as his playful, mystical, or "heroic" tendencies, but above all that outstanding quality of the primitive mind, which is its subjection to suprapersonal "powers," be they instincts, affects, superstitions, fantasies, magicians, witches, spirits, demons, or gods. Reduction leads back to the subjection of the primitive, which civilized man hopes he had escaped. And just as reduction makes a man

[66] Lévy-Bruhl, p. 57.

aware of his subjection to these "powers" and thus confronts him with a rather dangerous problem, so the synthetic treatment of the symbol brings him to the religious question, not so much to the problem of present-day religious creeds as to the religious problem of primitive man. In the face of the very real powers that dominate him, only an equally real fact can offer help and protection. No intellectual system, but direct experience only, can counterbalance the blind power of the instincts.

96   Over against the polymorphism of the primitive's instinctual nature there stands the regulating principle of individuation. Multiplicity and inner division are opposed by an integrative unity whose power is as great as that of the instincts. Together they form a pair of opposites necessary for self-regulation, often spoken of as nature and spirit. These conceptions are rooted in psychic conditions between which human consciousness fluctuates like the pointer on the scales.

97   The primitive mentality can be directly experienced by us only in the form of the infantile psyche that still lives in our memories. The peculiarities of this psyche are conceived by Freud, justly enough, as infantile sexuality, for out of this germinal state there develops the later, mature sexual being. Freud, however, derives all sorts of other mental peculiarities from this infantile germinal state, so that it begins to look as if the mind itself came from a preliminary sexual stage and were consequently nothing more than an offshoot of sexuality. Freud overlooks the fact that the infantile, polyvalent germinal state is not just a singularly perverse preliminary stage of normal and mature sexuality; it seems perverse because it is a preliminary stage not only of adult sexuality but also of the whole mental make-up of the individual. Out of the infantile germinal state there develops the complete adult man; hence the germinal state is no more exclusively sexual than is the mind of the grown man. In it are hidden not merely the beginnings of adult life, but also the whole ancestral heritage, which is of unlimited extent. This heritage includes not only instincts from the animal stage, but all those differentiations that have left hereditary traces behind them. Thus every child is born with an immense split in his make-up: on one side he is more or less like an animal, on the other side he is the final embodiment of an age-old and endlessly complicated sum of hereditary factors. This

split accounts for the tension of the germinal state and does much to explain the many puzzles of child psychology, which certainly has no lack of them.

98   If now, by means of a reductive procedure, we uncover the infantile stages of the adult psyche, we find as its ultimate basis germs containing on the one hand the later sexual being *in statu nascendi,* and on the other all those complicated preconditions of the civilized being. This is reflected most beautifully in children's dreams. Many of them are very simple "childish" dreams and are immediately understandable, but others contain possibilities of meaning that almost make one's head spin, and things that reveal their profound significance only in the light of primitive parallels. This other side is the mind *in nuce.* Childhood, therefore, is important not only because various warpings of instinct have their origin there, but because this is the time when, terrifying or encouraging, those far-seeing dreams and images appear before the soul of the child, shaping his whole destiny, as well as those retrospective intuitions which reach back far beyond the range of childhood experience into the life of our ancestors. Thus in the child-psyche the natural condition is already opposed by a "spiritual" one. It is recognized that man living in the state of nature is in no sense merely "natural" like an animal, but sees, believes, fears, worships things whose meaning is not at all discoverable from the conditions of his natural environment. Their underlying meaning leads us in fact far away from all that is natural, obvious, and easily intelligible, and quite often contrasts most sharply with the natural instincts. We have only to think of all those gruesome rites and customs against which every natural feeling rises in revolt, or of all those beliefs and ideas which stand in insuperable contradiction to the evidence of the facts. All this drives us to the assumption that the spiritual principle (whatever that may be) asserts itself against the merely natural conditions with incredible strength. One can say that this too is "natural," and that both have their origin in one and the same "nature." I do not in the least doubt this origin, but must point out that this "natural" something consists of a conflict between two principles, to which you can give this or that name according to taste, and that this opposition is the expression, and perhaps also the basis, of the tension we call psychic energy.

99   For theoretical reasons as well there must be some such tension of opposites in the child, otherwise no energy would be possible, for, as Heraclitus has said, "war is the father of all things." As I have remarked, this conflict can be understood as an opposition between the profoundly primitive nature of the newborn infant and his highly differentiated inheritance. The natural man is characterized by unmitigated instinctuality, by his being completely at the mercy of his instincts. The inheritance that opposes this condition consists of mnemonic deposits accruing from all the experience of his ancestors. People are inclined to view this hypothesis with scepticism, thinking that "inherited ideas" are meant. There is naturally no question of that. It is rather a question of inherited *possibilities* of ideas, "pathways" gradually traced out through the cumulative experience of our ancestors. To deny the inheritance of these pathways would be tantamount to denying the inheritance of the brain. To be consistent, such sceptics would have to assert that the child is born with the brain of an ape. But since it is born with a human brain, this must sooner or later begin to function in a human way, and it will necessarily begin at the level of the most recent ancestors. Naturally this functioning remains profoundly unconscious to the child. At first he is conscious only of the instincts and of what opposes these instincts— namely, his parents. For this reason the child has no notion that what stands in his way may be within himself. Rightly or wrongly it is projected on to the parents. This infantile prejudice is so tenacious that we doctors often have the greatest difficulty in persuading our patients that the wicked father who forbade everything is far more inside than outside themselves. Everything that works from the unconscious appears projected on others. Not that these others are wholly without blame, for even the worst projection is at least hung on a hook, perhaps a very small one, but still a hook offered by the other person.

100   Although our inheritance consists of psychological pathways, it was nevertheless mental processes in our ancestors that traced them. If they come to consciousness again in the individual, they can do so only in the form of other mental processes; and although these processes can become conscious only through individual experience and consequently appear as individual acquisitions, they are nevertheless pre-existent pathways which are

53

merely "filled out" by individual experience. Probably every "impressive" experience is just such a break-through into an old, previously unconscious river-bed.

101 These pre-existent pathways are hard facts, as indisputable as the historical fact of man having built a city out of his original cave. This development was made possible only by the formation of a community, and the latter only by the curbing of instinct. The curbing of instinct by mental and spiritual processes is carried through with the same force and the same results in the individual as in the history of mankind. It is a normative or, more accurately, a "nomothetical" [67] process, and it derives its power from the unconscious fact of these inherited pathways. The mind, as the active principle in the inheritance, consists of the sum of the ancestral minds, the "unseen fathers" [68] whose authority is born anew with the child.

102 The philosophical concept of mind as "spirit" has still not been able to free itself, as a term in its own right, from the overpowering bond of identity with the other connotation of spirit, namely "ghost." Religion, on the other hand, has succeeded in getting over the linguistic association with "spirits" by calling the supreme spiritual authority "God." In the course of the centuries this conception came to formulate a spiritual principle which is opposed to mere instinctuality. What is especially significant here is that God is conceived at the same time as the Creator of nature. He is seen as the maker of those imperfect creatures who err and sin, and at the same time he is their judge and taskmaster. Simple logic would say: if I make a creature who falls into error and sin, and is practically worthless because of his blind instinctuality, then I am manifestly a bad creator and have not even completed my apprenticeship. (As we know, this argument played an important role in Gnosticism.) But the religious point of view is not perturbed by this criticism; it asserts that the ways and intentions of God are inscrutable. Actually the Gnostic argument found little favour in history, because the unassailability of the God-concept obviously answers a vital need before which all logic pales. (It should be understood that we are speaking here not of God as a

67 ["Ordained by law."—EDITORS.]
68 Söderblom, *Das Werden des Gottesglaubens,* pp. 88ff. and 175ff.

54

Ding an sich, but only of a human conception which as such is a legitimate object of science.)

03   Although the God-concept is a spiritual principle *par excellence,* the collective metaphysical need nevertheless insists that it is at the same time a conception of the First Cause, from which proceed all those instinctual forces that are opposed to the spiritual principle. God would thus be not only the essence of spiritual light, appearing as the latest flower on the tree of evolution, not only the spiritual goal of salvation in which all creation culminates, not only the end and aim, but also the darkest, nethermost cause of Nature's blackest deeps. This is a tremendous paradox which obviously reflects a profound psychological truth. For it asserts the essential contradictoriness of one and the same being, a being whose innermost nature is a tension of opposites. Science calls this "being" energy, for energy is like a living balance between opposites. For this reason the God-concept, in itself impossibly paradoxical, may be so satisfying to human needs that no logic however justified can stand against it. Indeed the subtlest cogitation could scarcely have found a more suitable formula for this fundamental fact of inner experience.

04   It is not, I believe, superfluous to have discussed in considerable detail the nature of the opposites that underlie psychic energy.[69] Freudian theory consists in a causal explanation of the psychology of instinct. From this standpoint the spiritual principle is bound to appear only as an appendage, a by-product of the instincts. Since its inhibiting and restrictive power cannot be denied, it is traced back to the influence of education, moral authorities, convention and tradition. These authorities in their turn derive their power, according to the theory, from repression in the manner of a vicious circle. The spiritual principle is not recognized as an equivalent counterpart of the instincts.

The spiritual standpoint, on the other hand, is embodied in religious views which I can take as being sufficiently known. Freudian psychology appears threatening to this standpoint, but it is not more of a threat than materialism in general, whether scientific or practical. The one-sidedness of Freud's sexual

69 I have treated this same problem under other aspects and in another way in *Symbols of Transformation,* pars. 253, 680; and *Psychological Types* (1923 edn., p. 241) and the following section 3 (a).

theory is significant at least as a symptom. Even if it has no scientific justification, it has a moral one. It is undoubtedly true that instinctuality conflicts with our moral views most frequently and most conspicuously in the realm of sex. The conflict between infantile instinctuality and ethics can never be avoided. It is, it seems to me, the *sine qua non* of psychic energy. While we are all agreed that murder, stealing, and ruthlessness of any kind are obviously inadmissible, there is nevertheless what we call a "sexual question." We hear nothing of a murder question or a rage question; social reform is never invoked against those who wreak their bad tempers on their fellow men. Yet these things are all examples of instinctual behaviour, and the necessity for their suppression seems to us self-evident. Only in regard to sex do we feel the need of a question mark. This points to a doubt—the doubt whether our existing moral concepts and the legal institutions founded on them are really adequate and suited to their purpose. No intelligent person will deny that in this field opinion is sharply divided. Indeed, there would be no problem at all if public opinion were united about it. It is obviously a reaction against a too rigorous morality. It is not simply an outbreak of primitive instinctuality; such outbreaks, as we know, have never yet bothered themselves with moral laws and moral problems. There are, rather, serious misgivings as to whether our existing moral views have dealt fairly with the nature of sex. From this doubt there naturally arises a legitimate interest in any attempt to understand the nature of sex more truly and deeply, and this interest is answered not only by Freudian psychology but by numerous other researches of the kind. The special emphasis, therefore, that Freud has laid on sex could be taken as a more or less conscious answer to the question of the hour, and conversely, the acceptance that Freud has found with the public proves how well-timed his answer was.

106   An attentive and critical reader of Freud's writings cannot fail to remark how wide and flexible his concept of sexuality is. In fact it covers so much that one often wonders why in certain places the author uses a sexual terminology at all. His concept of sexuality includes not only the physiological sexual processes but practically every stage, phase, and kind of feeling or desire. This enormous flexibility makes his concept universally applicable, though not always to the advantage of the resulting

explanations. By means of this inclusive concept you can explain a work of art or a religious experience in exactly the same terms as an hysterical symptom. The absolute difference between these three things then drops right out of the picture. The explanation can therefore be only an apparent one for at least two of them. Apart from these inconveniences, however, it is psychologically correct to tackle the problem first from the sexual side, for it is just there that the unprejudiced person will find something to think about.

7   The conflict between ethics and sex today is not just a collision between instinctuality and morality, but a struggle to give an instinct its rightful place in our lives, and to recognize in this instinct a power which seeks expression and evidently may not be trifled with, and therefore cannot be made to fit in with our well-meaning moral laws. Sexuality is not mere instinctuality; it is an indisputably creative power that is not only the basic cause of our individual lives, but a very serious factor in our psychic life as well. Today we know only too well the grave consequences that sexual disturbances can bring in their train. We could call sexuality the spokesman of the instincts, which is why from the spiritual standpoint sex is the chief antagonist, not because sexual indulgence is in itself more immoral than excessive eating and drinking, avarice, tyranny, and other extravagances, but because the spirit senses in sexuality a counterpart equal and indeed akin to itself. For just as the spirit would press sexuality, like every other instinct, into its service, so sexuality has an ancient claim upon the spirit, which it once—in procreation, pregnancy, birth, and childhood—contained within itself, and whose passion the spirit can never dispense with in its creations. Where would the spirit be if it had no peer among the instincts to oppose it? It would be nothing but an empty form. A reasonable regard for the other instincts has become for us a self-evident necessity, but with sex it is different. For us sex is still problematical, which means that on this point we have not reached a degree of consciousness that would enable us to do full justice to the instinct without appreciable moral injury. Freud is not only a scientific investigator of sexuality, but also its champion; therefore, having regard to the great importance of the sexual problem, I recognize the moral justifica-

tion of his concept of sexuality even though I cannot accept it scientifically.

108   This is not the place to discuss the possible reasons for the present attitude to sex. It is sufficient to point out that sexuality seems to us the strongest and most immediate instinct,[70] standing out as *the* instinct above all others. On the other hand, I must also emphasize that the spiritual principle does not, strictly speaking, conflict with instinct as such but only with blind instinctuality, which really amounts to an unjustified preponderance of the instinctual nature over the spiritual. The spiritual appears in the psyche also as an instinct, indeed as a real passion, a "consuming fire," as Nietzsche once expressed it. It is not derived from any other instinct, as the psychologists of instinct would have us believe, but is a principle *sui generis,* a specific and necessary form of instinctual power. I have gone into this problem in a special study, to which I would refer the reader.[71]

109   Symbol-formation follows the road offered by these two possibilities in the human mind. Reduction breaks down all inappropriate and useless symbols and leads back to the merely natural course, and this causes a damming up of libido. Most of the alleged "sublimations" are compulsory products of this situation, activities cultivated for the purpose of using up the unbearable surplus of libido. But the really primitive demands are not satisfied by this procedure. If the psychology of this dammed-up condition is studied carefully and without prejudice, it is easy to discover in it the beginnings of a primitive form of religion, a religion of an individual kind altogether different from a dogmatic, collective religion.

110   Since the making of a religion or the formation of symbols is just as important an interest of the primitive mind as the satisfaction of instinct, the way to further development is logically given: escape from the state of reduction lies in evolving a religion of an individual character. One's true individuality then emerges from behind the veil of the collective personality, which would be quite impossible in the state of reduction since our instinctual nature is essentially collective. The development

[70] This is not the case with primitives, for whom the food question plays a far greater role.
[71] See my essay "Instinct and the Unconscious."

of individuality is also impossible, or at any rate seriously impeded, if the state of reduction gives rise to forced sublimations in the shape of various cultural activities, since these are in their essence equally collective. But, as human beings are for the most part collective, these forced sublimations are therapeutic products that should not be underestimated, because they help many people to bring a certain amount of useful activity into their lives. Among these cultural activities we must include the practice of a religion within the framework of an existing collective religion. The astonishing range of Catholic symbolism, for instance, has an emotional appeal which for many natures is absolutely satisfying. The immediacy of the relationship to God in Protestantism satisfies the mystic's passion for independence, while theosophy with its unlimited speculative possibilities meets the need for pseudo-Gnostic intuitions and caters to lazy thinking.

[1]   These organizations or systems are "symbola" ($\sigma\acute{v}\mu\beta o\lambda o\nu$ = confession of faith) which enable man to set up a spiritual counterpole to his primitive instinctual nature, a cultural attitude as opposed to sheer instinctuality. This has been the function of all religions. For a long time and for the great majority of mankind the symbol of a collective religion will suffice. It is perhaps only temporarily and for relatively few individuals that the existing collective religions have become inadequate. Wherever the cultural process is moving forward, whether in single individuals or in groups, we find a shaking off of collective beliefs. Every advance in culture is, psychologically, an extension of consciousness, a coming to consciousness that can take place only through discrimination. Therefore an advance always begins with individuation, that is to say with the individual, conscious of his isolation, cutting a new path through hitherto untrodden territory. To do this he must first return to the fundamental facts of his own being, irrespective of all authority and tradition, and allow himself to become conscious of his distinctiveness. If he succeeds in giving collective validity to his widened consciousness, he creates a tension of opposites that provides the stimulation which culture needs for its further progress.

[2]   This is not to say that the development of individuality is in all circumstances necessary or even opportune. Yet one may

well believe, as Goethe has said, that "the highest joy of man should be the growth of personality." There are large numbers of people for whom the development of individuality is the prime necessity, especially in a cultural epoch like ours, which is literally flattened out by collective norms, and where the newspaper is the real monarch of the earth. In my naturally limited experience there are, among people of maturer age, very many for whom the development of individuality is an indispensable requirement. Hence I am privately of the opinion that it is just the mature person who, in our times, has the greatest need of some further education in individual culture after his youthful education in school or university has moulded him on exclusively collective lines and thoroughly imbued him with the collective mentality. I have often found that people of riper years are in this respect capable of education to a most unexpected degree, although it is just those matured and strengthened by the experience of life who resist most vigorously the purely reductive standpoint.

113   Obviously it is in the youthful period of life that we have most to gain from a thorough recognition of the instinctual side. A timely recognition of sexuality, for instance, can prevent that neurotic suppression of it which keeps a man unduly withdrawn from life, or else forces him into a wretched and unsuitable way of living with which he is bound to come into conflict. Proper recognition and appreciation of normal instincts leads the young person into life and entangles him with fate, thus involving him in life's necessities and the consequent sacrifices and efforts through which his character is developed and his experience matured. For the mature person, however, the continued expansion of life is obviously not the right principle, because the descent towards life's afternoon demands simplification, limitation, and intensification—in other words, individual culture. A man in the first half of life with its biological orientation can usually, thanks to the youthfulness of his whole organism, afford to expand his life and make something of value out of it. But the man in the second half of life is oriented towards culture, the diminishing powers of his organism allowing him to subordinate his instincts to cultural goals. Not a few are wrecked during the transition from the biological to the cultural sphere.

Our collective education makes practically no provision for this transitional period. Concerned solely with the education of the young, we disregard the education of the adult, of whom it is always assumed—on what grounds who can say?—that he needs no more education. There is an almost total lack of guidance for this extraordinarily important transition from the biological to the cultural attitude, for the transformation of energy from the biological form into the cultural form. This transformation process is an individual one and cannot be enforced by general rules and maxims. It is achieved by means of the symbol. Symbol-formation is a fundamental problem that cannot be discussed here. I must refer the reader to Chapter V in my *Psychological Types,* where I have dealt with this question in detail.

IV. THE PRIMITIVE CONCEPTION OF LIBIDO

14   How intimately the beginnings of religious symbol-formation are bound up with a concept of energy is shown by the most primitive ideas concerning a magical potency, which is regarded both as an objective force and as a subjective state of intensity.

15   I will give some examples to illustrate this. According to the report of McGee, the Dakota Indians have the following conception of this "power." The sun is *wakonda,* not *the wakonda,* or *a wakonda,* but simply *wakonda.* The moon is *wakonda,* and so are thunder, lightning, stars, wind, etc. Men too, especially the shaman, are *wakonda,* also the demons of the elemental forces, fetishes, and other ritual objects, as well as many animals and localities of an especially impressive character. McGee says: "The expression [*wakonda*] can perhaps be rendered by the word 'mystery' better than any other, but even this concept is too narrow, because *wakonda* can equally well mean power, holy, old, greatness, alive, immortal." [72]

16   Similar to the use of *wakonda* by the Dakotas is that of *oki* by the Iroquois and of *manitu* by the Algonquins, with the abstract meaning of power or productive energy. *Wakonda* is the conception of a "diffused, all-pervasive, invisible, manipu-

[72] "The Siouan Indians—A Preliminary Sketch," p. 182; Lovejoy, "The Fundamental Concept of the Primitive Philosophy," p. 363.

lable and transferable life-energy and universal force." [73] The life of the primitive with all its interests is centred upon the possession of this power in sufficient amount.

[117]   Especially valuable is the observation that a concept like *manitu* occurs also as an exclamation when anything astonishing happens. Hetherwick [74] reports the same thing of the Yaos of central Africa, who cry *mulungu!* when they see something astonishing or incomprehensible. *Mulungu* means: (1) the soul of a man, which is called *lisoka* in life and becomes *mulungu* after death; (2) the entire spirit world; (3) the magically effective property or power inherent in any kind of object, such as the life and health of the body; (4) the active principle in everything magical, mysterious, inexplicable, and unexpected; and (5) the great spiritual power that has created the world and all life.

[118]   Similar to this is the *wong* concept of the Gold Coast. *Wong* can be a river, a tree, an amulet, or a lake, a spring, an area of land, a termite hill, crocodiles, monkeys, snakes, birds, etc. Tylor [75] erroneously interprets the *wong* force animistically as spirit or soul. But the way in which *wong* is used shows that it is a dynamic relation between man and objects.

[119]   The *churinga* [76] of the Australian aborigines is a similar energic concept. It means: (1) the ritual object; (2) the body of an individual ancestor (from whom the life force comes); (3) the mystical property of any object.

[120]   Much the same is the *zogo* concept of the Australian tribesmen of the Torres Strait, the word being used both as a noun

[73] Lovejoy, p. 365.
[74] "Some Animistic Beliefs among the Yaos of Central Africa."
[75] Tylor, *Primitive Culture*, II, pp. 176, 205.
[76] Spencer and Gillen, pp. 277f., where the following is reported of the *churinga* as a ritual object: "The native has a vague and undefined but still a very strong idea that any sacred object such as a Churinga, which has been handed down from generation to generation, is not only endowed with the magic power put into it when first it was made, but has gained some kind of virtue from every individual to whom it has belonged. A man who owns such a Churinga as this snake one will constantly rub it over with his hand, singing as he does so the Alcheringa history of the snake, and gradually comes to feel that there is some special association between him and the sacred object—that a virtue of some kind passes from it to him and also from him to it." Fetishes become charged with new power if left standing for some weeks or months near another strong fetish. Cf. Pechuël-Loesche, p. 366.

and an adjective. The Australian *arunquiltha* is a parallel concept of similar meaning, only it is the word for bad magic and for the evil spirit who likes to swallow the sun in an eclipse.[77] Of similar character is the Malayan *badi,* which also includes evil magical relationships.

121   The investigations of Lumholtz[78] have shown that the Mexican Huichols likewise have a fundamental conception of a power that circulates through men, ritual animals and plants (deer, mescal, corn, plumes, etc.).[79]

122   From the researches of Alice Fletcher among North American Indians it appears that the *wakan* concept is one of energic relationship similar to those already discussed. A man may become *wakan* through fasting, prayer, or visions. The weapons of a young man are *wakan;* they may not be touched by a woman (otherwise the libido runs backwards). For this reason the weapons are prayed to before battle (in order to make them powerful by charging them with libido). *Wakan* establishes the connection between the visible and the invisible, between the living and the dead, between the part and the whole of an object.

123   Codrington says of the Melanesian concept of *mana:* "The Melanesian mind is entirely possessed by the belief in a supernatural power or influence, called almost universally *mana.* This is what works to effect everything which is beyond the power of the ordinary man, outside the common processes of nature; it is present in the atmosphere of life, attaches itself to persons and to things, and is manifested by results which can only be ascribed to its operation. . . . It is a power or influence, not physical, and in a way supernatural; but it shows itself in physical force, or in any kind of power or influence which a man possesses. This *mana* is not fixed in anything, and can be conveyed in almost anything; but spirits, whether disembodied souls or supernatural beings, have it and can impart it; and it essentially belongs to personal beings to originate it, though it

---

[77] Spencer and Gillen, p. 458.   [78] *Unknown Mexico.*

[79] "When the Huichols, influenced by the law of participation, affirm the identity of corn, deer, *hikuli* [= mescal], and plumes, a classification has been established between their representatives. the governing principle of which is a common presence in these entities, or rather the circulation among them of a mystic power which is of supreme importance to the tribe." Lévy-Bruhl, p. 128.

may act through the medium of water, or a stone, or a bone." [80]

124   This description shows clearly that in the case of *mana*, as with the other concepts, we are dealing with a concept of energy which alone enables us to explain the remarkable fact of these primitive ideas. This is not to suggest that the primitive has an abstract idea of energy, but there can be no doubt that his concept is the preliminary concretistic stage of the abstract idea.

125   We find similar views in the *tondi* concept of the Bataks,[81] in the *atua* of the Maoris, in the *ani* or *han* of Ponape, the *kasinge* or *kalit* of Palau, the *anut* of Kusaie, the *yaris* of Tobi, the *ngai* of the Masai, the *andriamanitra* of the Malagasy, the *njom* of the Ekoi, etc. A complete survey is given by Söderblom in his book *Das Werden des Gottesglaubens*.

126   Lovejoy is of the opinion—with which I am in full agreement—that these concepts "are not primarily names for the 'supernormal' or the astonishing and certainly not for that which evokes awe, respect and love—but rather for the efficacious, the powerful, the productive." The concept in question really concerns the idea of "a diffused substance or energy upon the possession of which all exceptional power or ability or fecundity depends. The energy *is*, to be sure, terrible (under certain circumstances) and it is mysterious and incomprehensible; but it is so because it is vastly powerful, not because the things that manifest it are unusual and 'supernatural' or such as 'defeat reasonable expectation.'" The pre-animistic principle is the belief in "a force which is conceived as working according to quite regular and intelligible laws, a force which can be studied and controlled." [82] For these concepts Lovejoy suggests the term "primitive energetics."

127   Much that was taken by investigators animistically as spirit, demon, or numen really belongs to the primitive concept of energy. As I have already remarked, it is, in the strict sense, incorrect to speak of a "concept." "A concept of primitive philosophy," as Lovejoy calls it, is an idea obviously born of our own mentality; that is to say, for us *mana* would be a psy-

---

[80] Codrington, *The Melanesians*, p. 118. Seligmann, in his book *The Melanesians of British New Guinea*, so rich in valuable observations, speaks of *bariaua* (p. 446), which likewise belongs to the *mana* concept.
[81] Warnecke, *Die Religion der Batak*.
[82] Lovejoy, pp. 380f.

chological concept of energy, but for the primitive it is a psychic *phenomenon* that is perceived as something inseparable from the object. There are no abstract ideas to be found among primitives, not even, as a rule, simple concrete concepts, but only "representations." All primitive languages offer abundant proof of this. Thus *mana* is not a concept but a representation based on the perception of a "phenomenal" relationship. It is the essence of Lévy-Bruhl's *participation mystique*. In primitive speech only the fact of the relationship and the experience it evokes are indicated, as some of the above examples clearly show, not the nature or essence of that relationship, or of the principle determining it. The discovery of a suitable designation for the nature and essence of the unifying principle was reserved for a later level of culture, which substituted symbolic expressions.

128   In his classic study of *mana* Lehmann defines it as something "extraordinarily effective." The psychic nature of *mana* is especially emphasized by Preuss [83] and Röhr.[84] We cannot escape the impression that the primitive view of *mana* is a forerunner of our concept of psychic energy and, most probably, of energy in general.[85]

129   The basic conception of *mana* crops up again on the animistic level in personified form.[86] Here it is souls, demons, gods, who produce the extraordinary effect. As Lehmann rightly points out, nothing "divine" attaches to *mana*, so that one cannot see in *mana* the original form of an idea of God. Nonetheless, it cannot be denied that *mana* is a necessary or at least a very important precondition for the development of an idea of God, even though it may not be the most primitive of all

---

83 "Der Ursprung der Religion und Kunst."

84 "Das Wesen des Mana."

85 Cf. my discussion of the way in which Robert Mayer discovered the concept of energy: *Two Essays on Analytical Psychology*, pars. 106ff.

86 Seligmann (pp. 640ff.) reports observations which in my view show transitions of *mana* into animistic personifications. Such are the *labuni* of the Gelaria people of New Guinea. *Labuni* means "sending." It has to do with dynamic (magical) effects which emanate, or can be sent out, from the ovaries (?) of women who have borne children. *Labuni* look like "shadows," they use bridges to cross streams, change into animals, but otherwise possess no personality or definable form. Similar to this is the conception of the *ayik* which I observed among the Elgonyi, in northern Kenya.

preconditions. Another essential precondition is personification, for whose explanation other psychological factors must be adduced.

130   The almost universal incidence of the primitive concept of energy is a clear expression of the fact that even at early levels of human consciousness man felt the need to represent the sensed dynamism of psychic events in a concrete way. If, therefore, in our psychology we lay stress on the energic point of view, this is in accord with the psychic facts which have been graven on the mind of man since primordial times.

II

ON THE NATURE OF THE PSYCHE

ON THE NATURE OF THE PSYCHE [1]

1. The Unconscious in Historical Perspective

343   More clearly, perhaps, than any other science, psychology demonstrates the spiritual transition from the classical age to the modern. The history of psychology [2] up to the seventeenth century consists essentially in the enumeration of doctrines concerning the soul, but the soul was never able to get a word in as the object investigated. As the immediate datum of experience, it seemed so completely known to every thinker that he was convinced there could be no need of any further, let alone objective, experience. This attitude is totally alien to the modern standpoint, for today we are of the opinion that, over and above all subjective certainty, objective experience is needed to substantiate an opinion that lays claim to be scientific. Notwithstanding

---

1 [Originally published as "Der Geist der Psychologie," *Eranos-Jahrbuch 1946* (Zurich, 1947), pp. 385–490. This essay, revised and augmented, was republished as "Theoretische Überlegungen zum Wesen des Psychischen" in *Von den Wurzeln des Bewusstseins* (Psychologische Abhandlungen, IX; Zurich, 1954), pp. 497–608. The former version was translated by R. F. C. Hull as "The Spirit of Psychology" and published in *Spirit and Nature* (Papers from the Eranos Yearbooks, 1; New York, 1954; London, 1955), pp. 371–444. That translation is now further revised to bring it into conformity with the 1954 German version.—EDITORS.]
2 Hermann Siebeck, *Geschichte der Psychologie.*

this it is still difficult, even today, to apply the purely empirical or phenomenological standpoint consistently in psychology, because the original naïve idea that the soul, being the immediate datum of experience, was the best known of all knowables is one of our most deeply rooted convictions. Not only does every layman presume to an opinion, but every psychologist too—and not merely with reference to the subject but, what is of greater consequence, with reference to the object. He knows, or rather he thinks he knows, what is going on in another individual, and what is good for him. This is due less to a sovereign disregard of differences than to a tacit assumption that all individuals are alike. As a result, people incline unconsciously to a belief in the universal validity of subjective opinions. I mention this fact only to show that, in spite of the growing empiricism of the last three hundred years, the original attitude has by no means disappeared. Its continued existence only goes to prove how difficult is the transition from the old philosophical view to the modern empirical one.

344   Naturally it never occurred to the representatives of the old view that their doctrines were nothing but psychic phenomena, for it was naïvely assumed that with the help of intelligence or reason man could, as it were, climb out of his psychic condition and remove himself to one that was suprapsychic and rational. Even now, the doubt as to whether the statements of the human mind might not in the end be symptoms of certain psychic conditions is one that few people would consider seriously.[3] This question would be very much to the point, but it has such far-reaching and revolutionary consequences that we can understand only too well why both past and present have done their best to ignore it. We are still very far today from Nietzsche's view of philosophy, and indeed of theology, as an "ancilla psychologiae," for not even the psychologist is prepared to regard his statements, at least in part, as a subjectively conditioned confession. We can say that individuals are equal only in so far as they are in large measure unconscious—unconscious, that is, of their actual differences. The more unconscious a man is, the more he will conform to the general canon of psychic behaviour. But the more conscious he becomes of his individuality, the

[3] Actually this is true only of the old psychology. In recent times there has been a considerable change of standpoint.

more pronounced will be his difference from other subjects and the less he will come up to common expectations. Further, his reactions are much less predictable. This is due to the fact that an individual consciousness is always more highly differentiated and more extensive. But the more extensive it becomes the more differences it will perceive and the more it will emancipate itself from the collective rules, for the empirical freedom of the will grows in proportion to the extension of consciousness.

5   As the individual differentiation of consciousness proceeds, the objective validity of its views decreases and their subjectivity increases, at least in the eyes of the environment, if not in actual fact. For if a view is to be valid, it must have the acclaim of the greatest possible number, regardless of the arguments put forward in its favour. "True" and "valid" describe what the majority believe, for this confirms the equality of all. But a differentiated consciousness no longer takes it for granted that one's own preconceptions are applicable to others, and vice versa. This logical development had the consequence that in the seventeenth century—a century of great importance for the growth of science—psychology began to rise up by the side of philosophy, and it was Christian von Wolf (1679–1754) who was the first to speak of "empirical" or "experimental" psychology,[4] thus acknowledging the need to put psychology on a new footing. Psychology had to forgo the philosopher's rational definition of truth, because it gradually became clear that no philosophy had sufficient general validity to be uniformly fair to the diversity of individual subjects. And since on questions of principle, too, an indefinitely large number of different subjective statements was possible, whose validity in their turn could be maintained only subjectively, it naturally became necessary to abandon philosophical argument and to replace it by experience. Psychology thereupon turned into a natural science.

6   For the time being, however, philosophy retained its grip on the wide field of "rational" or "speculative" psychology, and only with the passage of the centuries could the latter gradually develop into a natural science. This process of change is not complete even today. Psychology, as a subject, still comes under

4 *Psychologia empirica* (1732).

the Philosophical Faculty in most universities and remains in the hands of professional philosophers, while "medical" psychology has still to seek refuge with the Medical Faculty. So officially the situation is still largely medieval, since even the natural sciences are only admitted as "Phil. II," under the cloak of Natural Philosophy.[5] Although it has been obvious for at least two hundred years that philosophy above all is dependent on psychological premises, everything possible was done to obscure the autonomy of the empirical sciences after it became clear that the discovery of the earth's rotation and the moons of Jupiter could no longer be suppressed. Of all the natural sciences, psychology has been the least able to win its independence.

347   This backwardness seems to me significant. The position of psychology is comparable with that of a psychic function which is inhibited by the conscious mind: only such components of it are admitted to exist as accord with the prevailing trend of consciousness. Whatever fails to accord is actually denied existence, in defiance of the fact that there are numerous phenomena or symptoms to prove the contrary. Anyone acquainted with these psychic processes knows with what subterfuges and self-deceiving manoeuvres one sets about splitting off the inconvenience. It is precisely the same with empirical psychology: as the discipline subordinate to a general philosophical psychology, experimental psychology is admitted as a concession to the empiricism of natural science, but is cluttered up with technical philosophical terms. As for psychopathology, it stays put in the Medical Faculty as a curious appendix to psychiatry. "Medical" psychology, as might be expected, finds little or no recognition in the universities.[6]

348   If I express myself somewhat drastically in this matter, it is with intent to throw into relief the position of psychology at the turn of the nineteenth and the beginning of the twentieth century. Wundt's standpoint is entirely representative of the situation as it then was—representative also because there emerged from his school a succession of notable psychologists who set the tone at the beginning of the twentieth century. In his *Outlines*

[5] In Anglo-Saxon countries there is the degree of "Doctor Scientiae," and psychology too enjoys greater independence.
[6] Recently these conditions have somewhat improved.

of Psychology, Wundt says: "Any psychical element that has disappeared from consciousness is to be called unconscious in the sense that we assume the possibility of its renewal, that is, its reappearance in the actual interconnection of psychical processes. Our knowledge of an element that has become unconscious does not extend beyond this possibility of its renewal. . . . For psychology, therefore, it has no meaning except as a disposition for the inception of future components. . . . Assumptions as to the state of the 'unconscious' or as to 'unconscious processes' of any kind . . . are *entirely unproductive for psychology.* There are, of course, physical concomitants of the psychical dispositions mentioned, of which some can be directly demonstrated, some inferred from various experiences." [7]

349   A representative of the Wundt school opines that "a psychic state cannot be described as psychic unless it has reached at least the threshold of consciousness." This argument assumes, or rather asserts, that only the conscious is psychic and that therefore everything psychic is conscious. The author happens to say a "psychic" state: logically he should have said a "state," for whether such a state is psychic is precisely the point at issue. Another argument runs: the simplest psychic fact is sensation, since it cannot be analysed into simpler facts. Consequently, that which precedes or underlies a sensation is never psychic, but only physiological. *Ergo,* there is no unconscious.

350   J. F. Herbart once said: "When a representation [idea] falls below the threshold of consciousness it goes on living in a latent way, continually striving to recross the threshold and to displace the other representations." As it stands, the proposition is undoubtedly incorrect, for unfortunately anything genuinely forgotten has no tendency to recross the threshold. Had Herbart said "complex" in the modern sense of the word instead of "representation," his proposition would have been absolutely right. We shall hardly be wrong in assuming that he really did mean something of the sort. In this connection, a philosophical opponent of the unconscious makes the very illuminating remark: "Once this be admitted, one finds oneself at the mercy of all manner of hypotheses concerning this unconscious life,

[7] Trans. by C. H. Judd, pp. 227-28, from *Grundriss der Psychologie.* (My italics.)

hypotheses which cannot be controlled by any observation." [8] It is evident that this thinker is not out to recognize facts, but that for him the fear of running into difficulties is decisive. And how does he know that these hypotheses cannot be controlled by observation? For him this is simply an *a priori*. But with Herbart's observation he does not deal at all.

351   I mention this incident not because of its positive significance but only because it is so thoroughly characteristic of the antiquated philosophical attitude towards empirical psychology. Wundt himself is of the opinion that, as regards the "so-called unconscious processes, it is not a question of unconscious psychic elements, but only of *more dimly conscious* ones," and that "for hypothetical unconscious processes we could substitute actually demonstrable or at any rate less hypothetical conscious processes." [9] This attitude implies a clear rejection of the unconscious as a psychological hypothesis. The cases of "double consciousness" he explains as "modifications of individual consciousness which very often occur continuously, in steady succession, and for which, by a violent misinterpretation of the facts, a plurality of individual consciousnesses is substituted." The latter, so Wundt argues, "would have to be simultaneously present in one and the same individual." This, he says, "is admittedly not the case." Doubtless it is hardly possible for two consciousnesses to express themselves simultaneously in a single individual in a blatantly recognizable way. That is why these states usually alternate. Janet has shown that while the one consciousness controls the head, so to speak, the other simultaneously puts itself into communication with the observer by means of a code of expressive manual movements.[10] Double consciousness may therefore very well be simultaneous.

352   Wundt thinks that the idea of a double consciousness, and hence of a "superconsciousness" and "subconsciousness" in Fechner's sense,[11] is a "survival from the psychological mysti-

---

8 Guido Villa, *Einleitung in die Psychologie der Gegenwart*, p. 339.
9 Wilhelm Wundt, *Grundzüge der physiologischen Psychologie*, III, p. 327.
10 Pierre Janet, *Automatisme psychologique*, pp. 243, 238ff.
11 Gustav Theodor Fechner, *Elemente der Psychophysik*, II, p. 438: ". . . the idea of a psychophysical threshold . . . gives a firm foundation to that of the unconscious generally. Psychology cannot abstract representations from unconscious perceptions, nor even from the effects of unconscious perceptions."

cism" of the Schelling school. He obviously boggles at an unconscious representation being one which nobody "has." [12] In
that case the word "representation" would naturally be obsolete
too, since it suggests a subject to whom something is present or
"presented." That is the basic reason for Wundt's rejection of the
unconscious. But we can easily get round this difficulty by speaking, not of "representations" or "perceptions," but of *contents*,
as I usually do. Here I must anticipate a point with which I
shall be dealing at some length later on, namely the fact that
something very like "representedness" or consciousness does
attach to unconscious contents, so that the possibility of an
unconscious subject becomes a serious question. Such a subject,
however, is not identical with the ego. That it was principally
the "representations" which were Wundt's *bête noire* is clear
also from his emphatic rejection of "inborn ideas." How literally
he takes this can be seen from the following: "If the new-born
animal really had an idea beforehand of all the actions it purposes to do, what a wealth of anticipated life-experiences would
lie stored in the human and animal instincts, and how incomprehensible it would seem that not man alone, but animals too,
acquire most things only through experience and practice!" [13]
There is, nevertheless, an inborn "pattern of behaviour" and
just such a treasure-house, not indeed of anticipated, but of
accumulated, life-experiences; only, it is not a question of "representations" but of sketches, plans, or images which, though
not actually "presented" to the ego, are yet just as real as Kant's
hundred thalers, which had been sewn into the lining of a jacket
and forgotten by the owner. Wundt might have remembered
Christian von Wolf, whom he himself mentions, and his distinction with regard to "unconscious" states which "can be inferred
only from what we find in our consciousness." [14]

53   To the category of "inborn ideas" also belong Adolf Bastian's
"elementary ideas," [15] by which we are to understand the funda-
mentally analogous forms of perception that are to be found
everywhere, therefore more or less what we know today as

[12] Ibid., p. 439.   [13] *Grundzüge der physiologischen Psychologie*, III, p. 328.
[14] Ibid., p. 326. Cited from Wolf's *Vernünftige Gedanken von Gott, der Welt, und der Seele des Menschen* (1719), §193.
[15] *Ethnische Elementargedanken in der Lehre vom Menschen* and *Der Mensch in der Geschichte*, I, pp. 166ff., 213ff.; II, pp. 24ff.

"archetypes." Wundt, of course, rejects this notion, under the delusion that he is dealing here with "representations" and not with "dispositions." He says: "The origination of one and the same phenomenon in different places is not absolutely impossible, but, from the standpoint of empirical psychology, it is in the highest degree unlikely." [16] He denies a "common psychic heritage of humanity" in this sense and repudiates the very idea of an intelligible myth-symbolism with the characteristic pronouncement that the supposition of a "system of ideas" hiding behind the myth is impossible.[17] The pedantic assumption that the unconscious is, of all things, a system of ideas would not hold water even in Wundt's day, let alone before or afterwards.

354   It would be incorrect to assume that the rejection of the idea of the unconscious in academic psychology at the turn of the century was anything like universal. That is by no means the case, for Fechner,[18] and after him Theodor Lipps, had given the unconscious a place of decisive importance.[19] Although for Lipps psychology is a "science of consciousness," he nevertheless speaks of "unconscious" perceptions and representations, which he regards as processes. "The nature or, more accurately, the idea of a 'psychic' process is not so much a conscious content or conscious experience as the psychic reality which must necessarily be thought to underlie the existence of such a process." [20] "Observation of conscious life persuades us that not only are unconscious perceptions and representations . . . at times to be found in us, but that psychic life *proceeds in that form most of the time, and only occasionally, at special points, does the agent within us reveal its presence directly, in appropriate images.*" [21]

[16] *Völkerpsychologie*, V, Part II, p. 459.   [17] Ibid., IV, Part I, p. 41.

[18] Cf. Fechner's remark that "the idea of a psychophysical threshold is of the utmost importance because it gives a firm foundation to that of the unconscious generally." He goes on: "Perceptions and representations in the state of unconsciousness have, of course, ceased to exist as real ones . . . but something continues in us, psychophysical activity," etc. (II, pp. 438f.). This conclusion is a little incautious, because the psychic process remains more or less the same whether conscious or not. A "representation" exists not only through its "representedness," but—and this is the main point—it also exists in its own psychic right.

[19] Cf. Lipps, "Der Begriff des Unbewussten," pp. 146ff.; and *Grundtatsachen des Seelenlebens*, pp. 125ff.

[20] *Leitfaden der Psychologie*, p. 64.   [21] Ibid., pp. 65f. (My italics.)

"Thus psychic life always goes far beyond the bounds of what is or may be present in us in the form of conscious contents or images."

55 Theodor Lipps' remarks in no wise conflict with our modern views, on the contrary they form the theoretical basis for the psychology of the unconscious in general. Nevertheless resistance to the hypothesis of the unconscious persisted for a long time afterwards. For instance it is characteristic that Max Dessoir, in his history of modern German psychology,[22] does not even mention C. G. Carus and Eduard von Hartmann.

2. The Significance of the Unconscious in Psychology

56 The hypothesis of the unconscious puts a large question-mark after the idea of the psyche. The soul, as hitherto postulated by the philosophical intellect and equipped with all the necessary faculties, threatened to emerge from its chrysalis as something with unexpected and uninvestigated properties. It no longer represented anything immediately known, about which nothing more remained to be discovered except a few more or less satisfying definitions. Rather it now appeared in strangely double guise, as both known and unknown. In consequence, the old psychology was thoroughly unseated and as much revolutionized [23] as classical physics had been by the discovery of radioactivity. These first experimental psychologists were in the same predicament as the mythical discoverer of the numerical sequence, who strung peas together in a row and

22 *Geschichte der neueren deutschen Psychologie.*

23 I reproduce here what William James says about the importance of the discovery of the unconscious psyche (*Varieties of Religious Experience,* p. 233): "I cannot but think that the most important step forward that has occurred in psychology since I have been a student of that science is the discovery, first made in 1886, that . . . there is not only the consciousness of the ordinary field, with its usual center and margin, but an addition thereto in the shape of a set of memories, thoughts, and feelings which are extramarginal and outside of the primary consciousness altogether, but yet must be classed as conscious facts of some sort, able to reveal their presence by unmistakable signs. I call this the most important step forward because, unlike the other advances which psychology has made, this discovery has revealed to us an entirely unsuspected peculiarity in the constitution of human nature. No other step forward which psychology has made can proffer any such claim as this." The discovery of 1886 to which James refers is the positing of a "subliminal consciousness" by Frederic W. H. Myers. See n. 47, infra.

simply went on adding another unit to those already present. When he contemplated the result, it looked as if there were nothing but a hundred identical units; but the numbers he had thought of only as names unexpectedly turned out to be peculiar entities with irreducible properties. For instance, there were even, uneven, and primary numbers; positive, negative, irrational, and imaginary numbers, etc.[24] So it is with psychology: if the soul is really only an idea, this idea has an alarming air of unpredictability about it—something with qualities no one would ever have imagined. One can go on asserting that the psyche is consciousness and its contents, but that does not prevent, in fact it hastens, the discovery of a background not previously suspected, a true matrix of all conscious phenomena, a preconsciousness and a postconsciousness, a superconsciousness and a subconsciousness. The moment one forms an idea of a thing and successfully catches one of its aspects, one invariably succumbs to the illusion of having caught the whole. One never considers that a total apprehension is right out of the question. Not even an idea posited as total is total, for it is still an entity on its own with unpredictable qualities. This self-deception certainly promotes peace of mind: the unknown is named, the far has been brought near, so that one can lay one's finger on it. One has taken possession of it, and it has become an inalienable piece of property, like a slain creature of the wild that can no longer run away. It is a magical procedure such as the primitive practises upon objects and the psychologist upon the psyche. He is no longer at its mercy, but he never suspects that the very fact of grasping the object conceptually gives it a golden opportunity to display all those qualities which would never have made their appearance had it not been imprisoned in a concept (remember the numbers!).

357   The attempts that have been made, during the last three hundred years, to grasp the psyche are all part and parcel of that tremendous expansion of knowledge which has brought the universe nearer to us in a way that staggers the imagination. The thousandfold magnifications made possible by the electron-microscope vie with the five hundred million light-year distances which the telescope travels. Psychology is still a long way from

24 A mathematician once remarked that everything in science was man-made except numbers, which had been created by God himself.

a development similar to that which the other natural sciences have undergone; also, as we have seen, it has been much less able to shake off the trammels of philosophy. All the same, every science is a function of the psyche, and all knowledge is rooted in it. The psyche is the greatest of all cosmic wonders and the *sine qua non* of the world as an object. It is in the highest degree odd that Western man, with but very few—and ever fewer— exceptions, apparently pays so little regard to this fact. Swamped by the knowledge of external objects, the subject of all knowledge has been temporarily eclipsed to the point of seeming non-existence.

8   The soul was a tacit assumption that seemed to be known in every detail. With the discovery of a possible unconscious psychic realm, man had the opportunity to embark upon a great adventure of the spirit, and one might have expected that a passionate interest would be turned in this direction. Not only was this not the case at all, but there arose on all sides an outcry against such an hypothesis. Nobody drew the conclusion that if the subject of knowledge, the psyche, were in fact a veiled form of existence not immediately accessible to consciousness, then all our knowledge must be incomplete, and moreover to a degree that we cannot determine. The validity of conscious knowledge was questioned in an altogether different and more menacing way than it had ever been by the critical procedures of epistemology. The latter put certain bounds to human knowledge in general, from which post-Kantian German Idealism struggled to emancipate itself; but natural science and common sense accommodated themselves to it without much difficulty, if they condescended to notice it at all. Philosophy fought against it in the interests of an antiquated pretension of the human mind to be able to pull itself up by its own bootstraps and know things that were right outside the range of human understanding. The victory of Hegel over Kant dealt the gravest blow to reason and to the further development of the German and, ultimately, of the European mind, all the more dangerous as Hegel was a psychologist in disguise who projected great truths out of the subjective sphere into a cosmos he himself had created. We know how far Hegel's influence extends today. The forces compensating this calamitous development personified themselves partly in the later Schelling, partly in Schopenhauer and Carus,

while on the other hand that unbridled "bacchantic God" whom Hegel had already scented in nature finally burst upon us in Nietzsche.

359   Carus' hypothesis of the unconscious was bound to hit the then prevailing trend of German philosophy all the harder, as the latter had apparently just got the better of Kantian criticism and had restored, or rather reinstated, the well-nigh godlike sovereignty of the human spirit—Spirit with a capital S. The spirit of medieval man was, in good and bad alike, still the spirit of the God whom he served. Epistemological criticism was on the one hand an expression of the modesty of medieval man, and on the other a renunciation of, or abdication from, the spirit of God, and consequently a modern extension and reinforcement of human consciousness within the limits of reason. Wherever the spirit of God is extruded from our human calculations, an unconscious substitute takes its place. In Schopenhauer we find the unconscious Will as the new definition of God, in Carus the unconscious, and in Hegel identification and inflation, the practical equation of philosophical reason with Spirit, thus making possible that intellectual juggling with the object which achieved such a horrid brilliance in his philosophy of the State. Hegel offered a solution of the problem raised by epistemological criticism in that he gave ideas a chance to prove their unknown power of autonomy. They induced that hybris of reason which led to Nietzsche's superman and hence to the catastrophe that bears the name of Germany. Not only artists, but philosophers too, are sometimes prophets.

360   I think it is obvious that all philosophical statements which transgress the bounds of reason are anthropomorphic and have no validity beyond that which falls to psychically conditioned statements. A philosophy like Hegel's is a self-revelation of the psychic background and, philosophically, a presumption. Psychologically, it amounts to an invasion by the unconscious. The peculiar high-flown language Hegel uses bears out this view: it is reminiscent of the megalomanic language of schizophrenics, who use terrific spellbinding words to reduce the transcendent to subjective form, to give banalities the charm of novelty, or pass off commonplaces as searching wisdom. So bombastic a terminology is a symptom of weakness, ineptitude, and lack of substance. But that does not prevent the latest German philos-

ophy from using the same crackpot power-words and pretending
that it is not unintentional psychology.

51   In the face of this elemental inrush of the unconscious into
the Western sphere of human reason, Schopenhauer and Carus
had no solid ground under them from which to develop and
apply their compensatory effect. Man's salutary submission to a
benevolent Deity, and the *cordon sanitaire* between him and
the demon of darkness—the great legacy of the past—remained
unimpaired with Schopenhauer, at any rate in principle, while
with Carus it was hardly touched at all, since he sought to tackle
the problem at the root by leading it away from the over-pre-
sumptuous philosophical standpoint towards that of psychology.
We have to close our eyes to his philosophical allure if we wish
to give full weight to his essentially psychological hypothesis.
He had at least come a step nearer to the conclusion we mentioned earlier, by trying to construct a world-picture that included the dark part of the soul. This structure still lacked
something whose unprecedented importance I would like to
bring home to the reader.

52   For this purpose we must first make it quite clear to ourselves
that all knowledge is the result of imposing some kind of order
upon the reactions of the psychic system as they flow into our
consciousness—an order which reflects the behaviour of a *meta-
psychic* reality, of that which is in itself real. If, as certain modern points of view, too, would have it, the psychic system
coincides and is identical with our conscious mind, then, in
principle, we are in a position to know everything that is capable
of being known, i.e., everything that lies within the limits of
the theory of knowledge. In that case there is no cause for
disquiet, beyond that felt by anatomists and physiologists when
contemplating the function of the eye or the organ of hearing.
But should it turn out that the psyche does *not* coincide with
consciousness, and, what is more, that it functions unconsciously
in a way similar to, or *different* from, the conscious portion of
it, then our disquiet must rise to the point of agitation. For it is
then no longer a question of general epistemological limits, but
of a flimsy threshold that separates us from the unconscious contents of the psyche. The hypothesis of the threshold and of the
unconscious means that the indispensable raw material of all
knowledge—namely psychic reactions—and perhaps even uncon-

scious "thoughts" and "insights" lie close beside, above, or below consciousness, separated from us by the merest "threshold" and yet apparently unattainable. We have no knowledge of how this unconscious functions, but since it is conjectured to be a psychic system it may possibly have everything that consciousness has, including perception, apperception, memory, imagination, will, affectivity, feeling, reflection, judgment, etc., all in subliminal form.[25]

363   Here we are faced with Wundt's objection that one cannot possibly speak of unconscious "perceptions," "representations," "feelings," much less of "volitional actions," seeing that none of these phenomena can be represented without an experiencing subject. Moreover, the idea of a threshold presupposes a mode of observation in terms of energy, according to which consciousness of psychic contents is essentially dependent upon their intensity, that is, their energy. Just as only a stimulus of a certain intensity is powerful enough to cross the threshold, so it may with some justice be assumed that other psychic contents too must possess a higher energy-potential if they are to get across. If they possess only a small amount of energy they remain subliminal, like the corresponding sense-perceptions.

364   As Lipps has already pointed out, the first objection is nullified by the fact that the psychic process remains essentially the same whether it is "represented" or not. Anyone who takes the view that the phenomena of consciousness comprise the whole psyche must go a step further and say that "representations which we do not have" [26] can hardly be described as "representa-

25 G. H. Lewes in *The Physical Basis of Mind* takes all this for granted. For instance, on p. 358, he says: "Sentience has various modes and degrees, such as Perception, Ideation, Emotion, Volition, which may be conscious, subconscious, or unconscious." On p. 363: "Consciousness and Unconsciousness are correlatives, both belonging to the sphere of Sentience. Every one of the unconscious processes is operant, changes the general state of the organism, and is capable of at once issuing in a discriminated sensation when the force which balances it is disturbed." On p. 367: "There are many involuntary actions of which we are distinctly conscious, and many voluntary actions of which we are at times subconscious and unconscious. . . . Just as the thought which at one moment passes unconsciously, at another consciously, is in itself the same thought . . . so the action which at one moment is voluntary, and at another involuntary, is itself the same action." Lewes certainly goes too far when he says (p. 373): "There is no real and essential distinction between voluntary and involuntary actions." Occasionally there is a world of difference.   26 Fechner, II, pp. 438f.

tions." He must also deny any psychic quality to what is left over. For this rigorous point of view the psyche can only have the phantasmagoric existence that pertains to the ephemeral phenomena of consciousness. This view does not square with common experience, which speaks in favour of a possible psychic activity without consciousness. Lipps' idea of the existence of psychic processes *an sich* does more justice to the facts. I do not wish to waste time in proving this point, but will content myself with saying that never yet has any reasonable person doubted the existence of psychic processes in a dog, although no dog has, to our knowledge, ever expressed consciousness of its psychic contents.[27]

3. *The Dissociability of the Psyche*

65   There is no *a priori* reason for assuming that unconscious processes must inevitably have a subject, any more than there is for doubting the reality of psychic processes. Admittedly the problem becomes difficult when we suppose unconscious acts of the will. If this is not to be just a matter of "instincts" and "inclinations," but rather of considered "choice" and "decision" which are peculiar to the will, then one cannot very well get round the need for a controlling subject to whom something is "represented." But that, by definition, would be to lodge a consciousness in the unconscious, though this is a conceptual operation which presents no great difficulties to the psychopathologist. He is familiar with a psychic phenomenon that seems to be quite unknown to "academic" psychology, namely the dissociation or dissociability of the psyche. This peculiarity arises from the fact that the connecting link between the psychic processes themselves is a very conditional one. Not only are unconscious processes sometimes strangely independent of the experiences of the conscious mind, but the conscious processes, too, show a distinct loosening or discreteness. We all know of the absurdities which are caused by complexes and are to be observed with the greatest accuracy in the association experiment. Just as the cases of double consciousness doubted by Wundt really do happen, so the cases where not the whole personality is split in half, but

[27] I am not counting "Clever Hans" [but cf. D. Katz, *Animals and Men,* 13ff.—Editors] and the dog who talked about the "primordial soul."

only smaller fragments are broken off, are much more probable and in fact more common. This is an age-old experience of mankind which is reflected in the universal supposition of a plurality of souls in one and the same individual. As the plurality of psychic components at the primitive level shows, the original state is one in which the psychic processes are very loosely knit and by no means form a self-contained unity. Moreover, psychiatric experience indicates that it often takes only a little to shatter the unity of consciousness so laboriously built up in the course of development and to resolve it back into its original elements.

366   This dissociability also enables us to set aside the difficulties that flow from the logically necessary assumption of a threshold of consciousness. If it is correct to say that conscious contents become subliminal, and therefore unconscious, through loss of energy, and conversely that unconscious processes become conscious through accretion of energy, then, if unconscious acts of volition are to be possible, it follows that these must possess an energy which enables them to achieve consciousness, or at any rate to achieve a state of secondary consciousness which consists in the unconscious process being "represented" to a subliminal subject who chooses and decides. This process must necessarily possess the amount of energy required for it to achieve such a consciousness; in other words, it is bound eventually to reach its "bursting point." [28] If that is so, the question arises as to why the unconscious process does not go right over the threshold and become perceptible to the ego. Since it obviously does not do this, but apparently remains suspended in the domain of a subliminal secondary subject, we must now explain why this subject, which is *ex hypothesi* charged with sufficient energy to become conscious, does not in its turn push over the threshold and articulate with the primary ego-consciousness. Psychopathology has the material needed to answer this question. This secondary consciousness represents a personality-component which has not been separated from ego-consciousness by mere accident, but which owes its separation to definite causes. Such a dissociation has two distinct aspects: in the one case, there is

[28] James, *Varieties of Religious Experience*, p. 232.

an originally conscious content that became subliminal because it was repressed on account of its incompatible nature: in the other case, the secondary subject consists essentially in a process that never entered into consciousness at all because no possibilities exist there of apperceiving it. That is to say, ego-consciousness cannot accept it for lack of understanding, and in consequence it remains for the most part subliminal, although, from the energy point of view, it is quite capable of becoming conscious. It owes its existence not to repression, but to subliminal processes that were never themselves conscious. Yet because there is in both cases sufficient energy to make it potentially conscious, the secondary subject does in fact have an effect upon ego-consciousness—indirectly or, as we say, "symbolically," though the expression is not a particularly happy one. The point is that the contents that appear in consciousness are at first *symptomatic*. In so far as we know, or think we know, what they refer to or are based on, they are *semiotic,* even though Freudian literature constantly uses the term "symbolic," regardless of the fact that in reality symbols always express something we do *not* know. The symptomatic contents are in part truly symbolic, being the indirect representatives of unconscious states or processes whose nature can be only imperfectly inferred and realized from the contents that appear in consciousness. It is therefore possible that the unconscious harbours contents so powered with energy that under other conditions they would be bound to become perceptible to the ego. In the majority of cases they are not repressed contents, but simply contents that are *not yet conscious* and have not been subjectively realized, like the demons and gods of the primitives or the "isms" so fanatically believed in by modern man. This state is neither pathological nor in any way peculiar; it is on the contrary the original norm, whereas the psychic wholeness comprehended in the unity of consciousness is an ideal goal that has never yet been reached.

367   Not without justice we connect consciousness, by analogy, with the sense functions, from the physiology of which the whole idea of a "threshold" is derived. The sound-frequencies perceptible to the human ear range from 20 to 20,000 vibrations per second; the wave-lengths of light visible to the eye range from 7700 to 3900 angstrom-units. This analogy makes it

conceivable that there is a lower as well as an upper threshold for psychic events, and that consciousness, the perceptual system par excellence, may therefore be compared with the perceptible scale of sound or light, having like them a lower and upper limit. Maybe this comparison could be extended to the psyche in general, which would not be an impossibility if there were "psychoid" processes at both ends of the psychic scale. In accordance with the principle "natura non facit saltus," such an hypothesis would not be altogether out of place.

368   In using the term "psychoid" I am aware that it comes into collision with the concept of the same name postulated by Driesch. By "the psychoid" he understands the directing principle, the "reaction determinant," the "prospective potency" of the germinal element. It is "the elemental agent discovered in action," [29] the "entelechy of real acting." [30] As Eugen Bleuler has aptly pointed out, Driesch's concept is more philosophical than scientific. Bleuler, on the other hand, uses the expression "die Psychoide" [31] as a collective term chiefly for the subcortical processes, so far as they are concerned with biological "adaptive functions." Among these Bleuler lists "reflexes and the development of species." He defines it as follows: "The *Psychoide* is the sum of all the purposive, mnemonic, and life-preserving functions of the body and central nervous system, with the exception of those cortical functions which we have always been accustomed to regard as psychic." [32] Elsewhere he says: "The body-psyche of the individual and the phylo-psyche together form a unity which, for the purposes of our present study, can most usefully be designated by the name *Psychoide*. Common to both *Psychoide* and psyche are . . . conation and the utilization of previous experiences . . . in order to reach the goal. This would include memory (engraphy and ecphoria) and association, hence something analogous to thinking." [33] Although it is clear what is meant by the "Psychoide," in practice it often gets confused with "psyche," as the above passage shows. But it is not at all clear why the subcortical functions it is supposed to

[29] Hans A. E. Driesch, *The Science and Philosophy of the Organism,* 1929, p. 221.
[30] Ibid., p. 281.
[31] In *Die Psychoide als Prinzip der organischen Entwicklung,* p. 11. A fem. sing. noun derived from *Psyche* ($\psi\upsilon\chi o\epsilon\iota\delta\eta\varsigma$ = 'soul-like').
[32] Ibid., p. 11.   [33] Ibid., p. 33.

designate should then be described as "quasi-psychic." The confusion obviously springs from the organological standpoint, still observable in Bleuler, which operates with concepts like "cortical soul" and "medullary soul" and has a distinct tendency to derive the corresponding psychic functions from these parts of the brain, although it is always the function that creates its own organ, and maintains or modifies it. The organological standpoint has the disadvantage that all the purposeful activities inherent in living matter ultimately count as "psychic," with the result that "life" and "psyche" are equated, as in Bleuler's use of the words "phylo-psyche" and "reflexes." It is extremely difficult, if not impossible, to think of a psychic function as independent of its organ, although in actual fact we experience the psychic process apart from its relation to the organic substrate. For the psychologist, however, it is the totality of these experiences that constitutes the object of investigation, and for this reason he must abjure a terminology borrowed from the anatomist. If I make use of the term "psychoid" [34] I do so with three reservations: firstly, I use it as an adjective, not as a noun; secondly, no psychic quality in the proper sense of the word is implied, but only a "quasi-psychic" one such as the reflex-processes possess; and thirdly, it is meant to distinguish a category of events from merely vitalistic phenomena on the one hand and from specifically psychic processes on the other. The latter distinction also obliges us to define more closely the nature and extent of the psyche, and of the unconscious psyche in particular.

369   If the unconscious can contain everything that is known to be a function of consciousness, then we are faced with the possibility that it too, like consciousness, possesses a subject, a sort of ego. This conclusion finds expression in the common and ever-recurring use of the term "subconsciousness." The latter term is certainly open to misunderstanding, as either it means what is "below consciousness," or it postulates a "lower" and

[34] I can avail myself of the word "psychoid" all the more legitimately because, although my use of the term derives from a different field of perception, it nevertheless seeks to delineate roughly the same group of phenomena that Bleuler had in mind. A. Busemann, in his book *Die Einheit der Psychologie* (p. 31), calls this non-differentiated psyche the "micropsychic."

secondary consciousness. At the same time this hypothetical "subconsciousness," which immediately becomes associated with a "superconsciousness," [35] brings out the real point of my argument: the fact, namely, that a second psychic system coexisting with consciousness—no matter what qualities we suspect it of possessing—is of absolutely revolutionary significance in that it could radically alter our view of the world. Even if no more than the perceptions taking place in such a second psychic system were carried over into ego-consciousness, we should have the possibility of enormously extending the bounds of our mental horizon.

370   Once we give serious consideration to the hypothesis of the unconscious, it follows that our view of the world can be but a provisional one; for if we effect so radical an alteration in the subject of perception and cognition as this dual focus implies, the result must be a world view very different from any known before. This holds true only if the hypothesis of the unconscious holds true, which in turn can be verified only if unconscious contents can be changed into conscious ones—if, that is to say, the disturbances emanating from the unconscious, the effects of spontaneous manifestations, of dreams, fantasies, and complexes, can successfully be integrated into consciousness by the interpretative method.

4. Instinct and Will

371   Whereas, in the course of the nineteenth century, the main concern was to put the unconscious on a philosophical footing,[36] towards the end of the century various attempts were made in different parts of Europe, more or less simultaneously and independently of one another, to understand the unconscious experimentally or empirically. The pioneers in this field were

[35] Especial exception is taken to this "superconsciousness" by people who have come under the influence of Indian philosophy. They usually fail to appreciate that their objection only applies to the hypothesis of a "subconsciousness," which ambiguous term I avoid using. On the other hand my concept of the *unconscious* leaves the question of "above" or "below" completely open, as it embraces both aspects of the psyche.

[36] Cf. in particular Eduard von Hartmann, *Philosophie des Unbewussten* (1869).

Pierre Janet [37] in France and Sigmund Freud [38] in the old Austria. Janet made himself famous for his investigation of the formal aspect, Freud for his researches into the content of psychogenic symptoms.

2   I am not in a position here to describe in detail the transformation of unconscious contents into conscious ones, so must content myself with hints. In the first place, the structure of psychogenic symptoms was successfully explained on the hypothesis of unconscious processes. Freud, starting from the symptomatology of the neuroses, also made out a plausible case for dreams as the mediators of unconscious contents. What he elicited as contents of the unconscious seemed, on the face of it, to consist of elements of a personal nature that were quite capable of consciousness and had therefore been conscious under other conditions. It seemed to him that they had "got repressed" on account of their morally incompatible nature. Hence, like forgotten contents, they had once been conscious and had become subliminal, and more or less irrecoverable, owing to a countereffect exerted by the attitude of the conscious mind. By suitably concentrating the attention and letting oneself be guided by associations—that is, by the pointers still existing in consciousness—the associative recovery of lost contents went forward as in a mnemo-technical exercise. But whereas forgotten contents were irrecoverable because of their lowered threshold-value, repressed contents owed their relative irrecoverability to a check exercised by the conscious mind.

73   This initial discovery logically led to the interpretation of the unconscious as a phenomenon of repression which could be understood in personalistic terms. Its contents were lost elements that had once been conscious. Freud later acknowledged the continued existence of archaic vestiges in the form of primitive modes of functioning, though even these were explained personalistically. On this view the unconscious psyche appears as a subliminal appendix to the conscious mind.

37 An appreciation of his work is to be found in Jean Paulus, *Le Problème de l'hallucination et l'évolution de la psychologie d'Esquirol à Pierre Janet.*
38 In this connection we should also mention the important Swiss psychologist Théodore Flournoy and his chef d'œuvre *Des Indes à la Planète Mars* (1900). Other pioneers were W. B. Carpenter (*Principles of Mental Physiology,* 1874) and G. H. Lewes (*Problems of Life and Mind,* 1873–79). For Frederic W. H. Myers see nn. 23 and 47.

374   The contents that Freud raised to consciousness are those which are the most easily recoverable because they have the capacity to become conscious and were originally conscious. The only thing they prove with respect to the unconscious psyche is that there is a psychic limbo somewhere beyond consciousness. Forgotten contents which are still recoverable prove the same. This would tell us next to nothing about the nature of the unconscious psyche did there not exist an undoubted link between these contents and the instinctual sphere. We think of the latter as physiological, as in the main a function of the glands. The modern theory of internal secretions and hormones lends the strongest support to this view. But the theory of human instincts finds itself in a rather delicate situation, because it is uncommonly difficult not only to define the instincts conceptually, but even to establish their number and their limitations.[39] In this matter opinions diverge. All that can be ascertained with any certainty is that the instincts have a physiological and a psychological aspect.[40] Of great use for descriptive purposes is Pierre Janet's view of the "partie supérieure et inférieure d'une fonction." [41]

375   The fact that all the psychic processes accessible to our observation and experience are somehow bound to an organic substrate indicates that they are articulated with the life of the organism as a whole and therefore partake of its dynamism—in other words, they must have a share in its instincts or be in a certain sense the results of the action of those instincts. This is not to say that the psyche derives exclusively from the instinctual sphere and hence from its organic substrate. The psyche as such cannot be explained in terms of physiological chemistry, if only because, together with "life" itself, it is the only "natural factor" capable of converting statistical organizations which are

[39] This indistinctness and blurring of the instincts may, as E. N. Marais has shown in his experiments with apes (*The Soul of the White Ant*, p. 429), have something to do with the superior learning-capacity prevailing over the instincts, as is obviously the case with man too. On the question of instincts see L. Szondi, *Experimentelle Triebdiagnostik* and *Triebpathologie*.
[40] "The instincts are physiological and psychic dispositions which . . . cause the organism to move in a clearly defined direction" (W. Jerusalem, *Lehrbuch der Psychologie*, p. 188). From another point of view Oswald Külpe describes instinct as "a fusion of feelings and organ sensations" (*Outlines of Psychology*, p. 322, modified).   [41] *Les Névroses*, pp. 384ff.

subject to natural law into "higher" or "unnatural" states, in opposition to the rule of entropy that runs throughout the inorganic realm. How life produces complex organic systems from the inorganic we do not know, though we have direct experience of how the psyche does it. Life therefore has a specific law of its own which cannot be deduced from the known physical laws of nature. Even so, the psyche is to some extent dependent upon processes in the organic substrate. At all events, it is highly probable that this is so. The instinctual base governs the *partie inférieure* of the function, while the *partie supérieure* corresponds to its predominantly "psychic" component. The *partie inférieure* proves to be the relatively unalterable, automatic part of the function, and the *partie supérieure* the voluntary and alterable part.[42]

76   The question now arises: when are we entitled to speak of "psychic" and how in general do we define the "psychic" as distinct from the "physiological"? Both are life-phenomena, but they differ in that the functional component characterized as the *partie inférieure* has an unmistakably physiological aspect. Its existence or nonexistence seems to be bound up with the hormones. Its functioning has a compulsive character: hence the designation "drive." Rivers asserts that the "all-or-none reaction" [43] is natural to it, i.e., the function acts altogether or not at all, which is specific of compulsion. On the other hand the *partie supérieure*, which is best described as psychic and is moreover sensed as such, has lost its compulsive character, can be subjected to the will [44] and even applied in a manner contrary to the original instinct.

77   From these reflections it appears that the psychic is an

[42] Janet says (p. 384): "It seems that we must distinguish in every function inferior and superior parts. When a function has been in use for a long time it contains parts which are very old, work very easily, and are represented by very distinct and specialized organs. . . . these are the inferior parts of the function. But it is my opinion that in every function there are also superior parts which consist in the function's adaptation to more recent and much less usual circumstances, and are represented by organs which are differentiated in a markedly lesser degree." But the highest part of the function consists "in its adaptation to the particular circumstances of the present moment, the moment at which we have to use it."   [43] W. H. R. Rivers, "Instinct and the Unconscious."
[44] This formulation is purely psychological and has nothing to do with the philosophical problem of indeterminism.

emancipation of function from its instinctual form and so from the compulsiveness which, as sole determinant of the function, causes it to harden into a mechanism. The psychic condition or quality begins where the function loses its outer and inner determinism and becomes capable of more extensive and freer application, that is, where it begins to show itself accessible to a will motivated from other sources. At the risk of anticipating my programme, I cannot refrain from pointing out that if we delimit the psyche from the physiological sphere of instinct at the bottom, so to speak, a similar delimitation imposes itself at the top. For, with increasing freedom from sheer instinct the *partie supérieure* will ultimately reach a point at which the intrinsic energy of the function ceases altogether to be oriented by instinct in the original sense, and attains a so-called "spiritual" form. This does not imply a substantial alteration of the motive power of instinct, but merely a different mode of its application. The meaning or purpose of the instinct is not unambiguous, as the instinct may easily mask a sense of direction other than biological, which only becomes apparent in the course of development.

378   Within the psychic sphere the function can be deflected through the action of the will and modified in a great variety of ways. This is possible because the system of instincts is not truly harmonious in composition and is exposed to numerous internal collisions. One instinct disturbs and displaces the other, and, although taken as a whole it is the instincts that make individual life possible, their blind compulsive character affords frequent occasion for mutual injury. Differentiation of function from compulsive instinctuality, and its voluntary application, are of paramount importance in the maintenance of life. But this increases the possibility of collision and produces cleavages—the very dissociations which are forever putting the unity of consciousness in jeopardy.

379   In the psychic sphere, as we have seen, the will influences the function. It does this by virtue of the fact that it is itself a form of energy and has the power to overcome another form. In this sphere which I define as psychic, the will is in the last resort motivated by instincts—not, of course, absolutely, otherwise it would not be a will, which by definition must have a certain freedom of choice. "Will" implies a certain amount of energy

freely disposable by the psyche. There must be such amounts of disposable libido (or energy), or modifications of the functions would be impossible, since the latter would then be chained to the instincts—which are in themselves extremely conservative and correspondingly unalterable—so exclusively that no variations could take place, unless it were organic variations. As we have already said, the motivation of the will must in the first place be regarded as essentially biological. But at the (permitting such an expression) upper limit of the psyche, where the function breaks free from its original goal, the instincts lose their influence as movers of the will. Through having its form altered, the function is pressed into the service of other determinants or motivations, which apparently have nothing further to do with the instincts. What I am trying to make clear is the remarkable fact that the will cannot transgress the bounds of the psychic sphere: it cannot coerce the instinct, nor has it power over the spirit, in so far as we understand by this something more than the intellect. Spirit and instinct are by nature autonomous and both limit in equal measure the applied field of the will. Later I shall show what seems to me to constitute the relation of spirit to instinct.

Just as, in its lower reaches, the psyche loses itself in the organic-material substrate, so in its upper reaches it resolves itself into a "spiritual" form about which we know as little as we do about the functional basis of instinct. What I would call the psyche proper extends to all functions which can be brought under the influence of a will. Pure instinctuality allows no consciousness to be conjectured and needs none. But because of its empirical freedom of choice, the will needs a supraordinate authority, something like a consciousness of itself, in order to modify the function. It must "know" of a goal different from the goal of the function. Otherwise it would coincide with the driving force of the function. Driesch rightly emphasizes: "There is no willing without knowing." [45] Volition presupposes a choosing subject who envisages different possibilities. Looked at from this angle, psyche is essentially conflict between blind instinct and will (freedom of choice). Where instinct predominates, *psychoid*

[45] *Die "Seele" als elementarer Naturfaktor,* p. 80. "Individualized stimuli inform . . . the 'primary knower' of the abnormal state, and now this 'knower' not only *wants* a remedy but *knows* what it is" (p. 82).

processes set in which pertain to the sphere of the unconscious as elements incapable of consciousness. The psychoid process is not the unconscious as such, for this has a far greater extension. Apart from psychoid processes, there are in the unconscious ideas and volitional acts, hence something akin to conscious processes; [46] but in the instinctual sphere these phenomena retire so far into the background that the term "psychoid" is probably justified. If, however, we restrict the psyche to acts of the will, we arrive at the conclusion that psyche is more or less identical with consciousness, for we can hardly conceive of will and freedom of choice without consciousness. This apparently brings us back to where we always stood, to the axiom *psyche = consciousness*. What, then, has happened to the postulated psychic nature of the unconscious?

5. *Conscious and Unconscious*

381   This question, regarding the nature of the unconscious, brings with it the extraordinary intellectual difficulties with which the psychology of the unconscious confronts us. Such difficulties must inevitably arise whenever the mind launches forth boldly into the unknown and invisible. Our philosopher sets about it very cleverly, since, by his flat denial of the unconscious, he clears all complications out of his way at one sweep. A similar quandary faced the physicist of the old school, who believed exclusively in the wave theory of light and was then led to the discovery that there are phenomena which can be explained only by the particle theory. Happily, modern physics has shown the psychologist that it can cope with an apparent *contradictio in adiecto*. Encouraged by this example, the psychologist may be emboldened to tackle this controversial problem without having the feeling that he has dropped out of the world of natural science altogether. It is not a question of his *asserting* anything, but of constructing a *model* which opens up a promising and useful field of inquiry. A model does not assert that something *is* so, it simply illustrates a particular mode of observation.

382   Before we scrutinize our dilemma more closely, I would like

[46] Cf. sec. 6 below, "The Unconscious as a Multiple Consciousness."

to clarify one aspect of the concept of the unconscious. The unconscious is not simply the unknown, it is rather the *unknown psychic;* and this we define on the one hand as all those things in us which, if they came to consciousness, would presumably differ in no respect from the known psychic contents, with the addition, on the other hand, of the psychoid system, of which nothing is known directly. So defined, the unconscious depicts an extremely fluid state of affairs: everything of which I know, but of which I am not at the moment thinking; everything of which I was once conscious but have now forgotten; everything perceived by my senses, but not noted by my conscious mind; everything which, involuntarily and without paying attention to it, I feel, think, remember, want, and do; all the future things that are taking shape in me and will sometime come to consciousness: all this is the content of the unconscious. These contents are all more or less capable, so to speak, of consciousness, or were once conscious and may become conscious again the next moment. Thus far the unconscious is "a fringe of consciousness," as William James put it.[47] To this marginal phenomenon, which is born of alternating shades of light and darkness, there also belong the Freudian findings we have already noted. But, as I say, we must also include in the unconscious the psychoid functions that are not capable of consciousness and of whose existence we have only indirect knowledge.

³3 We now come to the question: in what state do psychic

---

[47] James speaks also of a "transmarginal field" of consciousness and identifies it with the "subliminal consciousness" of F. W. H. Myers, one of the founders of the British Society for Psychical Research (cf. *Proceedings S.P.R.,* VII, 1892, pp. 298ff., and William James, "Frederic Myers' Service to Psychology," ibid., XVII, 1901, pp. 13ff.). Concerning the "field of consciousness" James says (*Varieties of Religious Experience,* p. 232): "The important fact which this 'field' formula commemorates is the indetermination of the margin. Inattentively realized as is the matter which the margin contains, it is nevertheless there, and helps both to guide our behavior and to determine the next movement of our attention. It lies around us like a 'magnetic field' inside of which our center of energy turns like a compass needle as the present phase of consciousness alters into its successor. Our whole past store of memories floats beyond this margin, ready at a touch to come in; and the entire mass of residual powers, impulses, and knowledges that constitute our empirical self stretches continuously beyond it. So vaguely drawn are the outlines between what is actual and what is only potential at any moment of our conscious life, that it is always hard to say of certain mental elements whether we are conscious of them or not."

contents find themselves when not related to the conscious ego? (This relation constitutes all that can be called consciousness.) In accordance with "Occam's razor," *entia praeter necessitatem non sunt multiplicanda* ("principles are not to be multiplied beyond the necessary"), the most cautious conclusion would be that, except for the relation to the conscious ego, nothing is changed when a content becomes unconscious. For this reason I reject the view that momentarily unconscious contents are only physiological. The evidence is lacking, and apart from that the psychology of neurosis provides striking proofs to the contrary. One has only to think of the cases of double personality, *automatisme ambulatoire,* etc. Both Janet's and Freud's findings indicate that everything goes on functioning in the unconscious state just as though it were conscious. There is perception, thinking, feeling, volition, and intention, just as though a subject were present; indeed, there are not a few cases—e.g., the double personality above mentioned—where a second ego actually appears and vies with the first. Such findings seem to show that the unconscious is in fact a "subconscious." But from certain experiences—some of them known already to Freud—it is clear that the state of unconscious contents is not quite the same as the conscious state. For instance, feeling-toned complexes in the unconscious do not change in the same way that they do in consciousness. Although they may be enriched by associations, they are not corrected, but are conserved in their original form, as can easily be ascertained from the continuous and uniform effect they have upon the conscious mind. Similarly, they take on the uninfluenceable and compulsive character of an automatism, of which they can be divested only if they are made conscious. This latter procedure is rightly regarded as one of the most important therapeutic factors. In the end such complexes—presumably in proportion to their distance from consciousness—assume, by self-amplification, an archaic and mythological character and hence a certain numinosity, as is perfectly clear in schizophrenic dissociations. Numinosity, however, is wholly outside conscious volition, for it transports the subject into the state of rapture, which is a state of will-less surrender.

384   These peculiarities of the unconscious state contrast very strongly with the way complexes behave in the conscious mind. Here they can be corrected: they lose their automatic character

and can be substantially transformed. They slough off their mythological envelope, and, by entering into the adaptive process going forward in consciousness, they personalize and rationalize themselves to the point where a dialectical discussion becomes possible.[48] Evidently the unconscious state is different after all from the conscious. Although at first sight the process continues in the unconscious as though it were conscious, it seems, with increasing dissociation, to sink back to a more primitive (archaic-mythological) level, to approximate in character to the underlying instinctual pattern, and to assume the qualities which are the hallmarks of instinct: automatism, non-susceptibility to influence, all-or-none reaction, and so forth. Using the analogy of the spectrum, we could compare the lowering of unconscious contents to a displacement towards the red end of the colour band, a comparison which is especially edifying in that red, the blood colour, has always signified emotion and instinct.[49]

385   The unconscious is accordingly a different medium from the conscious. In the near-conscious areas there is not much change, because here the alternation of light and shadow is too rapid. But it is just this no man's land which is of the greatest value in supplying the answer to the burning question of whether psyche = consciousness. It shows us how relative the unconscious state is, so relative, indeed, that one feels tempted to make use of a concept like "the subconscious" in order to define the darker part of the psyche. But consciousness is equally relative, for it embraces not only consciousness as such, but a whole scale of intensities of consciousness. Between "I do this" and "I am conscious of doing this" there is a world of difference, amounting sometimes to outright contradiction. Consequently there is a consciousness in which unconsciousness predominates, as well as a consciousness in which self-consciousness predominates. This paradox becomes immediately intelligible when we realize that there is no conscious content which can with absolute certainty

48 In schizophrenic dissociation there is no such change in the conscious state, because the complexes are received not into a complete but into a fragmentary consciousness. That is why they so often appear in the original archaic state.

49 Red had a *spiritual* significance for Goethe, but that was in accord with his creed of feeling. Here we may conjecture the alchemical and Rosicrucian background, e.g., the red tincture and the carbuncle. Cf. *Psychology and Alchemy,* pars. 335, 454, 552.

be said to be totally conscious,[50] for that would necessitate an unimaginable totality of consciousness, and that in turn would presuppose an equally unimaginable wholeness and perfection of the human mind. So we come to the paradoxical conclusion that there is no conscious content which is not in some other respect unconscious. Maybe, too, there is no unconscious psychism which is not at the same time conscious.[51] The latter proposition is more difficult to prove than the first, because our ego, which alone could verify such an assertion, is the point of reference for all consciousness and has no such association with unconscious contents as would enable it to say anything about their nature. So far as the ego is concerned, they are, for all practical purposes, unconscious: which is not to say that they are not conscious to it in another respect, for the ego may know these contents under one aspect but not know them under another aspect, when they cause disturbances of consciousness. Besides, there are processes with regard to which no relation to the conscious ego can be demonstrated and which yet seem to be "represented" or "quasi-conscious." Finally, there are cases where an unconscious ego and hence a second consciousness are present, as we have already seen, though these are the exceptions.[52]

386   In the psychic sphere, the compulsive pattern of behaviour gives way to variations of behaviour which are conditioned by experience and by volitional acts, that is, by conscious processes. With respect to the psychoid, reflex-instinctual state, therefore, the psyche implies a loosening of bonds and a steady recession of mechanical processes in favour of "selected" modifications. This selective activity takes place partly inside consciousness and

[50] As already pointed out by E. Bleuler: *Naturgeschichte der Seele und ihres Bewusstwerdens*, pp. 300f.

[51] With the explicit exception of the psychoid unconscious, as this includes things which are not capable of consciousness and are only "quasi-psychic."

[52] In this connection I would mention that C. A. Meier associates observations of this kind with similar phenomena in physics. He says: "The relationship of complementarity between conscious and unconscious urges upon us yet another physical parallel, namely the need for a strict application of the 'principle of correspondence.' This might provide the key to the 'strict logic' of the unconscious (the logic of probability) which we so often experience in analytical psychology and which makes us think of an 'extended state of consciousness.' "—"Moderne Physik—Moderne Psychologie," p. 360.

partly outside it, i.e., without reference to the conscious ego, and hence unconsciously. In the latter case the process is "quasi-conscious," *as if* it were "represented" and conscious.

7   As there are no sufficient grounds for assuming that a second ego exists in every individual or that everyone suffers from dissociation of personality, we have to discount the idea of a second ego-consciousness as a source of voluntary decisions. But since the existence of highly complex, quasi-conscious processes in the unconscious has been shown, by the study of psychopathology and dream psychology, to be uncommonly probable, we are for better or worse driven to the conclusion that although the state of unconscious contents is not identical with that of conscious ones, it is somehow very "like" it. In these circumstances there is nothing for it but to suppose something midway between the conscious and unconscious state, namely an approximative consciousness. As we have immediate experience only of a reflected state, which is *ipso facto* conscious and known because it consists essentially in relating ideas or other contents to an ego-complex that represents our empirical personality, it follows that any other kind of consciousness—either without an ego or without contents—is virtually unthinkable. But there is no need to frame the question so absolutely. On a somewhat more primitive human level, ego-consciousness loses much of its meaning, and consciousness is accordingly modified in a characteristic way. Above all, it ceases to be reflected. And when we observe the psychic processes in the higher vertebrates and particularly in domestic animals, we find phenomena resembling consciousness which nevertheless do not allow us to conjecture the existence of an ego. As we know from direct experience, the light of consciousness has many degrees of brightness, and the ego-complex many gradations of emphasis. On the animal and primitive level there is a mere "luminosity," differing hardly at all from the glancing fragments of a dissociated ego. Here, as on the infantile level, consciousness is not a unity, being as yet uncentred by a firmly-knit ego-complex, and just flickering into life here and there wherever outer or inner events, instincts, and affects happen to call it awake. At this stage it is still like a chain of islands or an archipelago. Nor is it a fully integrated whole even at the higher and highest stages; rather, it is capable of indefinite expansion. Gleaming islands, indeed whole continents,

can still add themselves to our modern consciousness—a phenomenon that has become the daily experience of the psychotherapist. Therefore we would do well to think of ego-consciousness as being surrounded by a multitude of little luminosities.

6. The Unconscious as a Multiple Consciousness

388   The hypothesis of multiple luminosities rests partly, as we have seen, on the quasi-conscious state of unconscious contents and partly on the incidence of certain images which must be regarded as symbolical. These are to be found in the dreams and visual fantasies of modern individuals, and can also be traced in historical records. As the reader may be aware, one of the most important sources for symbolical ideas in the past is alchemy. From this I take, first and foremost, the idea of the *scintillae*—sparks—which appear as visual illusions in the "arcane substance." [53] Thus the *Aurora consurgens*, Part II, says: "Scito quod terra foetida cito recipit scintillulas albas" (Know that the foul earth quickly receives white sparks).[54] These sparks Khunrath explains as "radii atque scintillae" of the "anima catholica," the world-soul, which is identical with the spirit of God.[55] From this interpretation it is clear that certain of the alchemists had already divined the psychic nature of these luminosities. They were seeds of light broadcast in the chaos, which Khunrath calls "mundi futuri seminarium" (the seed plot of a world to come).[56]

[53] *Psychology and Alchemy*, pars. 352, 472. [And *Myst. Coniunctionis*, pars. 42ff.]
[54] *Artis auriferae* (1593), I, p. 208. Said to be a quotation from Morienus (cf. infra, par. 394), repeated by Mylius, *Philosophia reformata* (1622), p. 146. On p. 149 he adds "scintillas aureas."
[55] "Variae eius radii atque scintillae, per totius ingentem materiei primae massae molem hinc inde dispersae ac dissipatae: inque mundi partibus disiunctis etiam et loco et corporis mole, necnon circumscriptione, postea separatis . . . unius Animae universalis scintillae nunc etiam inhabitantes" (Its divers rays and sparks are dispersed and dissipated throughout the immense bulk of the whole mass of the *prima materia:* the sparks of the one universal soul now inhabiting those disunited parts of the world which were later separated from the place and mass of the body, and even from its circumference). Khunrath, *Amphitheatrum sapientiae aeternae solius verae* (1604), pp. 195f., 198.
[56] Ibid., p. 197. Cf. the Gnostic doctrine of the Seeds of Light harvested by the Virgin of Light, and the Manichaean doctrine of the light-particles which have to

One such spark is the human mind.[57] The arcane substance—the watery earth or earthy water (*limus:* mud) of the World Essence —is "universally animated" by the "fiery spark of the soul of the world," in accordance with the Wisdom of Solomon 1 : 7: "For the Spirit of the Lord filleth the world." [58] In the "Water of the Art," in "our Water," which is also the chaos,[59] there are to be found the "fiery sparks of the soul of the world as pure *Formae Rerum essentiales*." [60] These *formae* [61] correspond to the Platonic Ideas, from which one could equate the *scintillae* with the archetypes on the assumption that the Forms "stored up in a supracelestial place" are a philosophical version of the latter. One would have to conclude from these alchemical visions that the archetypes have about them a certain effulgence or quasi-consciousness, and that numinosity entails luminosity. Paracelsus seems to have had an inkling of this. The following is taken from his *Philosophia sagax:* "And as little as aught can exist in man without the divine numen, so little can aught exist in man without the natural lumen. A man is made perfect by numen and lumen and these two alone. Everything springs from these two, and these two are in man, but without them man is nothing, though they can be without man." [62] In confirmation of this Khunrath writes: "There be . . . *Scintillae Animae Mundi igneae, Luminis nimirum Naturae,* fiery sparks of the world soul, i.e., of the light of nature . . . dispersed or sprinkled in and throughout the structure of the great world

be taken into one's body as ritual food, at a sort of Eucharist when melons were eaten. The earliest mention of this idea seems to be the καρπιστής (Irenaeus, *Contra haereses*, I, 2, 4). Concerning the melons see M.-L. von Franz, "Der Traum des Descartes."

57 "Mens humani animi scintilla altior et lucidior" (The mind of the human soul is a higher and more luminous spark). *Amphitheatrum*, p. 63.

58 Khunrath, *Von hylealischen . . . Chaos* (1597), p. 63.

59 As synonyms, Khunrath mentions (p. 216) "forma aquina, pontica, limus terrae Adamae, Azoth, Mercurius" (a form watery and sea-like, the slime of the earth of Adama, etc.). [*Adama* is Hebrew for 'earth.'—EDITORS.] 60 Ibid., p. 216.

61 The "formae scintillaeve Animae Mundi" (forms or sparks of the world soul) are also called by Khunrath (p. 189) "rationes seminariae Naturae specificae" (the seed-ideas of Nature, the origin of species), thus reproducing an ancient idea. In the same way he calls the *scintilla* "Entelechia" (p. 65).

62 *Paracelsus: Sämtliche Werke,* ed. by Karl Sudhoff, XII, p. 231; *Bücher und Schrifften . . . Paracelsi . . . ,* ed. by Johannes Huser, X, p. 206.

into all fruits of the elements everywhere." [63] The sparks come from the "Ruach Elohim," the Spirit of God.[64] Among the *scintillae* he distinguishes a "scintilla perfecta Unici Potentis ac Fortis," which is the elixir and hence the arcane substance itself.[65] If we may compare the sparks to the archetypes, it is evident that Khunrath lays particular stress on one of them. This One is also described as the Monad and the Sun, and they both indicate the Deity. A similar image is to be found in the letter of Ignatius of Antioch to the Ephesians, where he writes of the coming of Christ: "How, then, was he manifested to the world? A star shone in heaven beyond the stars, and its light was unspeakable, and its newness caused astonishment, and all the other stars, with the sun and moon, gathered in chorus round this star. . . ." [66] Psychologically, the One Scintilla or Monad is to be regarded as a symbol of the self—an aspect I mention only in passing.

388   The sparks have a clear psychological meaning for Dorn. He says: "Thus little by little he will come to see with his mental eyes a number of sparks shining day by day and more and more and growing into such a great light that thereafter all things needful to him will be made known." [67] This light is the *lumen naturae* which illuminates consciousness, and the *scintillae* are germinal luminosities shining forth from the darkness of the unconscious. Dorn, like Khunrath, owes much to Paracelsus, with whom he concurs when he supposes an "invisibilem solem plurimis incognitum" in man (an invisible sun unknown to many).[68] Of this natural light innate in man Dorn says: "For the life, the light of men,[69] shineth in us, albeit dimly, and as

63 *Von hylealischen Chaos*, p. 94.   64 Ibid., p. 249.

65 Ibid., p. 54. In this he agrees with Paracelsus, who calls the *lumen naturae* the Quintessence, extracted from the four elements by God himself. (Sudhoff, XII, pp. 36, 304.)

66 Ch. XIX, 1ff. (trans. by Lake in *The Apostolic Fathers*, I, p. 193).

67 "Sic paulatim scintillas aliquot magis ac magis indies perlucere suis oculis mentalibus percipiet, ac in tantam excrescere lucem, ut successivo tempore quaevis innotescant, quae sibi necessaria fuerint." Gerhard Dorn, "Speculativae philosophiae," in *Theatrum chemicum*, I (1602), p. 275.

68 "Sol est invisibilis in hominibus, in terra vero visibilis, tamen ex uno et eodem sole sunt ambo" (The sun is invisible in men, but visible in the world, yet both are of one and the same sun). Ibid., p. 308.

69 "Et vita erat lux hominum. Et lux in tenebris lucet" (And the life was the light of men. And the light shineth in the darkness). John 1 : 4, 5.

though in darkness. It is not to be extracted from us, yet it is in us and not of us, but of Him to Whom it belongs, Who deigns to make us his dwelling-place. . . . He has implanted that light in us that we may see in its light the light of Him Who dwells in inaccessible light, and that we may excel His other creatures; in this wise we are made like unto Him, that He has given us a spark of His light. Thus the truth is to be sought not in ourselves, but in the image of God which is within us." [70]

Thus the one archetype emphasized by Khunrath is known also to Dorn as the *sol invisibilis* or *imago Dei*. In Paracelsus the *lumen naturae* comes primarily from the "astrum" or "sydus," the "star" in man.[71] The "firmament" (a synonym for the star) is the natural light.[72] Hence the "corner-stone" of all truth is "Astronomia," which is "a mother to all the other arts. . . . After her beginneth the divine wisdom, after her beginneth the light of nature," [73] even the "most excellent Religiones" hang upon Astronomia.[74] For the star "desireth to drive man toward great wisdom . . . that he may appear wondrous in the light of nature, and the mysteria of God's wondrous work be discovered and revealed in their grandeur." [75] Indeed, man himself is an "Astrum": "not by himself alone, but for ever and ever with all apostles and saints; each and every one is an astrum, the heaven a star . . . therefore saith also the Scripture: ye are lights of the world." [76] "Now as in the star lieth the whole natural light, and from it man taketh the same like food from the earth into which he is born, so too must he be born into the star." [77] Also the

---

[70] "Lucet in nobis licet obscure vita lux hominum tanquam in tenebris, quae non ex nobis quaerenda, tamen in et non a nobis, sed ab eo cuius est, qui etiam in nobis habitationem facere dignatur. . . . Hic eam lucem plantavit in nobis, ut in eius lumine qui lucem inaccessibilem inhabitat, videremus lumen; hoc ipso quoque caeteras eius praecelleremus creaturas; illi nimirum similes hac ratione facti, quod scintillam sui luminis dederit nobis. Est igitur veritas non in nobis quaerenda, sed in imagine Dei quae in nobis est." "Philosophia meditativa," *Theatrum chemicum*, I, p. 460.

[71] Sudhoff, XII, p. 23: "That which is in the light of nature, the same is the working of the star." (Huser, X, p. 19.)

[72] *Philosophia sagax*, Huser, X, p. 1 (Sudhoff, XII, p. 3).

[73] Ibid., pp. 3f. (pp. 5f.).

[74] The apostles are "Astrologi": ibid., p. 23 (p. 27).   [75] Ibid., p. 54 (p. 62).

[76] Ibid., p. 344 (p. 386). The last sentence refers to Matthew 5 : 14: "Vos estis lux mundi."   [77] Ibid., p. 409 (pp. 456f.).

animals have the natural light which is an "inborn spirit." [78]
Man at his birth is "endowed with the perfect light of nature." [79]
Paracelsus calls it "primum ac optimum thesaurum, quem
naturae Monarchia in se claudit" [80] (the first and best treasure
which the monarchy of nature hides within itself), in this con-
curring with the world-wide descriptions of the One as the pearl
of great price, the hidden treasure, the "treasure hard to attain,"
etc. The light is given to the "inner man" or the inner body
(*corpus subtile*, breath-body), as the following passage makes
clear:

A man may come forth with sublimity and wisdom from his outer
body, because the same wisdom and understanding which he
needeth for this are coaeval with this body and are the inner man; [81]
thus he may live and not as an outer man. For such an inner man is
eternally transfigured and true, and if in the mortal body he appeareth not perfect, yet he appeareth perfect after the separation of the
same. That which we now tell of is called *lumen naturae* and is
eternal. God hath given it to the inner body, that it may be ruled by
the inner body and in accordance with reason . . . for the light of
nature alone is reason and no other thing . . . the light is that
which giveth faith . . . to each man God hath given sufficient pre-
destined light that he err not. . . . But if we are to describe the
origin of the inner man or body, mark that all inner bodies be but
one body and one single thing in all men, albeit divided in accordance with the well-disposed numbers of the body, each one different.
And should they all come together, it is but one light, and one
reason. [82]

391   "Moreover, the light of nature is a light that is lit from the
Holy Ghost and goeth not out, for it is well lit . . . and the
light is of a kind that desireth to burn, [83] and the longer [it burns]

[78] ". . . like the cocks which crow the coming weather and the peacocks the death
of their master . . . all this is of the inborn spirit and is the light of nature."
Fragmenta medica, cap. "De morbis somnii," Huser, V, p. 130 (Sudhoff, IX, p. 361).
[79] *Liber de generatione hominis*, VIII, p. 172 (I, p. 300).
[80] *De vita longa*, ed. by Adam von Bodenstein (1562), Lib. V, c. ii.
[81] *Philosophia sagax*, X, p. 341 (XII, p. 382): "Now it is clear that all the human
wisdom of the earthly body lieth in the light of nature." It is "man's light of
eternal wisdom": ibid., p. 395 (p. 441).
[82] *Liber de generatione hominis*, VIII, pp. 171f. (I, pp. 299f.).
[83] "I am come to send fire on the earth; and what will I, if it be already kindled?"
Luke (AV) 12 : 49.

to shine the more, and the longer the greater . . . therefore in the light of nature is a fiery longing to enkindle." [84] It is an "invisible" light: "Now it follows that in the invisible alone hath man his wisdom, his art from the light of nature." [85] Man is "a prophet of the natural light." [86] He "learns" the *lumen naturae* through dreams,[87] among other things. "As the light of nature cannot speak, it buildeth shapes in sleep from the power of the word" (of God).[88]

392   I have allowed myself to dwell at some length on Paracelsus and to cite a number of authentic texts, because I wanted to give the reader a rough idea of the way in which this author conceives the *lumen naturae*. It strikes me as significant, particularly in regard to our hypothesis of a multiple consciousness and its phenomena, that the characteristic alchemical vision of sparks scintillating in the blackness of the arcane substance should, for Paracelsus, change into the spectacle of the "interior firmament" and its stars. He beholds the darksome psyche as a star-strewn night sky, whose planets and fixed constellations represent the archetypes in all their luminosity and numinosity.[89] The starry vault of heaven is in truth the open book of cosmic projection, in which are reflected the mythologems, i.e., the archetypes. In this vision astrology and alchemy, the two classical functionaries of the psychology of the collective unconscious, join hands.

393   Paracelsus was directly influenced by Agrippa von Nettesheim,[90] who supposes a "luminositas sensus naturae." From this "gleams of prophecy came down to the four-footed beasts, the birds, and other living creatures," and enabled them to foretell future things.[91] He bases the *sensus naturae* on the authority of

---

[84] *Fragmenta cum libro de fundamento sapientiae*, IX, p. 448 (XIII, pp. 325f.).
[85] *Philosophia sagax*, X, p. 46 (XII, p. 53).   [86] Ibid., p. 79 (p. 94).
[87] *Practica in scientiam divinationis*, X, p. 438 (XII, p. 488).
[88] *Liber de Caducis*, IV, p. 274 (VIII, p. 298).
[89] In the *Hieroglyphica* of Horapollo the starry sky signifies God as ultimate Fate, symbolized by a "5," presumably a quincunx. [Trans. by George Boas, p. 66.— Editors.]   [90] *Alchemical Studies*, index, *s.v.* "Agrippa."
[91] Cornelius Heinrich Agrippa von Nettesheim, *De occulta philosophia* (1533), p. lxix: "Nam iuxta Platonicorum doctrinam, est rebus inferioribus vis quaedam insita, per quam magna ex parte cum superioribus conveniunt, unde etiam animalium taciti consensus cum divinis corporibus consentire videntur, atque his viribus eorum corpora et affectus affici." (For according to the doctrine of the

Gulielmus Parisiensis, who is none other than William of Auvergne (G. Alvernus; d. 1249), bishop of Paris from about 1228, author of many works, which influenced Albertus Magnus among others. Alvernus says that the *sensus naturae* is superior to the perceptive faculty in man, and he insists that animals also possess it.[92] The doctrine of the *sensus naturae* is developed from the idea of the all-pervading world-soul with which another Gulielmus Parisiensis was much concerned, a predecessor of Alvernus by name of Guillaume de Conches [93] (1080–1154), a Platonist scholastic who taught in Paris. He identified the *anima mundi*, this same *sensus naturae*, with the Holy Ghost, just as Abelard did. The world-soul is a natural force which is responsible for all the phenomena of life and the psyche. As I have shown elsewhere, this view of the *anima mundi* ran through the whole tradition of alchemy in so far as Mercurius was interpreted now as *anima mundi* and now as the Holy Ghost.[94] In view of the importance of alchemical ideas for the psychology of the unconscious, it may be worth our while to devote a little time to a very illuminating variant of this spark symbolism.

394   Even more common than the spark-motif is that of the fish's eyes, which have the same significance. I said above that a Morienus passage is given by the authors as the source for the "doctrine" of the *scintillae*. This passage is, indeed, to be found in the treatise of Morienus Romanus. But it reads: ". . . Purus laton tamdiu decoquitur, donec veluti oculi piscium elucescat . . ." [95] Here too the saying seems to be a citation from a still earlier source. In later authors these fish's eyes are always cropping up. There is a variant in Sir George Ripley, stating that on the "desiccation of the sea" a substance is left behind

---

Platonists there is in the lower things a certain virtue through which they agree in large measure with the higher; whence it would seem that the tacit consent of animals is in agreement with divine bodies, and that their bodies and affections are touched by these virtues), etc.

[92] Lynn Thorndike, *History of Magic and Experimental Science*, II, pp. 348f.

[93] François Picavet, *Essais sur l'histoire générale et comparée des théologies et des philosophies médiévales,* p. 207.

[94] Cf. *Psychology and Alchemy*, pars. 172, 265, 506, and pars. 446, 518.

[95] "Liber de compositione Alchemiae," in *Artis auriferae*, II, p. 32: "The pure lato is cooked until it has the lustre of fish's eyes." Thus, by the authors themselves, the *oculi piscium* are interpreted as *scintillae*.

which "glitters like a fish's eye" [96]—an obvious allusion to the gold and the sun (God's eye). Hence it is not to be wondered at if an alchemist [97] of the seventeenth century uses the words of Zacharias 4 : 10 as a motto for his edition of Nicholas Flamel: "Et videbunt lapidem stanneum in manu Zorobabel. Septem isti oculi sunt Domini, qui discurrunt in universam terram" (And . . . they shall see the tin plummet in the hand of Zorobabel. These are the seven eyes of the Lord that run to and fro through the whole earth).[98] These seven eyes are evidently the seven planets which, like the sun and moon, are the eyes of God, never resting, ubiquitous and all-seeing. The same motif is probably at the bottom of the many-eyed giant Argus. He is nicknamed Πανόπτης, 'the All-Seeing,' and is supposed to symbolize the starry heavens. Sometimes he is one-eyed, sometimes four-eyed, sometimes hundred-eyed, and even myriad-eyed (μυριωπός). Besides which he never sleeps. Hera transferred the eyes of Argus Panoptes to the peacock's tail.[99] Like the guardian Argus, the constellation of the Dragon is also given an all-surveying position in the Aratus citations of Hippolytus. He is there described as the one "who from the height of the Pole looks down upon all things and sees all things, so that nothing that happens shall be hidden from him." [100] This dragon is sleepless, because the Pole "never sets." Often he appears to be confused with the sun's serpentine passage through the sky: "C'est pour ce motif qu'on dispose parfois les signes du zodiaque entre les circonvolutions du reptile," says Cumont.[101] Sometimes the serpent bears six signs of the zodiac upon his back.[102] As Eisler has remarked, on account of the time symbolism the all-seeing quality of the dragon

[96] *Opera omnia chemica* (1649), p. 159.

[97] Eirenaeus Orandus, *Nicholas Flamel: His Exposition of the Hieroglyphicall Figures etc.* (1624).

[98] Zach. 3 : 9 is also relevant: ". . . upon one stone there are seven eyes." (Both DV.)

[99] This mythologem is of importance in interpreting the "cauda pavonis."

[100] "Τετάχθαι γὰρ νομίζουσι κατὰ τὸν ἀρκτικὸν πόλον τὸν Δράκοντα, τὸν ὄφιν, ἀπὸ τοῦ ὑψηλοτάτου πόλου πάντα ἐπιβλέποντα καὶ πάντα ἐφορῶντα, ἵνα μηδὲν τῶν πραττομένων αὐτὸν λάθῃ." *Elenchos*, IV, 47, 2, 3. Cf. Legge, I, p. 109.

[101] F. Cumont, *Textes et monuments figurés relatifs aux mystères de Mithra*, I, p. 80.

[102] "Προσέταξε τὸν αὐτὸν δράκοντα βαστάζειν ἐξ ζῴδια ἐπὶ τοῦ νώτου αὐτοῦ."—Pitra, ed., *Analecta sacra*, V, p. 300. Quoted in Robert Eisler, *Weltenmantel und Himmelszelt* (1910), II, p. 389, 5.

is transferred to Chronos, whom Sophocles names "ὁ πάντ᾽ ὁρῶν Χρόνος," while in the memorial tablet for those who fell at Chaeronea he is called "πανεπίσκοπος δαίμων." [103] The Uroboros has the meaning of eternity (αἰών) and cosmos in Horapollo. The identification of the All-Seeing with Time probably explains the eyes on the wheels in Ezekiel's vision (A.V., 1 : 18: "As for their rings, they were so high that they were dreadful; and their rings were full of eyes round about them four"). We mention this identification because of its special importance: it indicates the relation between the *mundus archetypus* of the unconscious and the "phenomenon" of Time—in other words, it points to the *synchronicity* of archetypal events, of which I shall have more to say towards the end of this paper.

395 From Ignatius Loyola's autobiography, which he dictated to Loys Gonzales,[104] we learn that he used to see a bright light, and sometimes this apparition seemed to him to have the form of a serpent. It appeared to be full of shining eyes, which were yet no eyes. At first he was greatly comforted by the beauty of the vision, but later he recognized it to be an evil spirit.[105] This vision sums up all the aspects of our optic theme and presents a most impressive picture of the unconscious with its disseminated luminosities. One can easily imagine the perplexity which a medieval man would be bound to feel when confronted by such an eminently "psychological" intuition, especially as he had no dogmatic symbol and no adequate patristic allegory to come to his rescue. But, as a matter of fact, Ignatius was not so very wide of the mark, for multiple eyes are also a characteristic of Purusha, the Hindu Cosmic Man. The Rig-Veda (10. 90) says: "Thousand-headed is Purusha, thousand-eyed, thousand-footed. He encompasses the earth on every side and rules over the ten-finger space." [106] Monoïmos the Arabian, according to Hip-

[103] Eisler, p. 388. "The All-seeing Chronos" and "the all-beholding daemon."
[104] *The Testament of Ignatius Loyola*, trans. by E. M. Rix, p. 72.
[105] Ignatius also had the vision of a "res quaedam rotunda tanquam ex auro et magna" that floated before his eyes: a thing round, as if made of gold, and great. He interpreted it as Christ appearing to him like a *sun*. Philipp Funk, *Ignatius von Loyola*, pp. 57, 65, 74, 112.
[106] [Trans. derived from various sources. As Coomaraswamy explains in the *Journal of the American Oriental Society*, LVI (1946), 145–61, "the ten-finger space" (lit. "the ten-fingered") refers "macrocosmically to the distance between sky and earth and microcosmically to the space between the top of the head and

polytus, taught that the First Man (Ἄνθρωπος) was a single Monad (μία μονάς), not composed (ἀσύνθετος), indivisible (ἀδιαίρετος), and at the same time composed (συνθετή) and divisible (διαιρετή). This Monad is the iota or dot (μία κεραία), and this tiniest of units which corresponds to Khunrath's one *scintilla* has "many faces" (πολυπρόσωπος) and "many eyes'" (πολυόμματος).[107] Monoïmos bases himself here mainly on the prologue to the Gospel of St. John! Like Purusha, his First Man is the universe (ἄνθρωπος εἶναι τὸ πᾶν).[108]

396   Such visions must be understood as introspective intuitions that somehow capture the state of the unconscious and, at the same time, as assimilations of the central Christian idea. Naturally enough, the motif has the same meaning in modern dreams and fantasies, where it appears as the star-strewn heavens, as stars reflected in dark water, as nuggets of gold or golden sand scattered in black earth,[109] as a regatta at night, with lanterns on the dark surface of the sea, as a solitary eye in the depths of the sea or earth, as a parapsychic vision of luminous globes, and so on. Since consciousness has always been described in terms derived from the behaviour of light, it is in my view not too much to assume that these multiple luminosities correspond to tiny conscious phenomena. If the luminosity appears in monadic form as a single star, sun, or eye, it readily assumes the shape of a mandala and must then be interpreted as the self. It has nothing whatever to do with "double consciousness," because there is no indication of a dissociated personality. On the contrary, the symbols of the self have a "uniting" character.[110]

---

the chin" of a man. He continues: "I therefore consider it shown that what RV 10. 90. 1 . . . means is that Purusha, making the whole earth his footstool, fills the entire universe, and rules over it by means of the powers of vision, etc., that proceed from his face, and to which man's own powers of vision, etc., are analogous; this face, whether of God or man, being . . . itself an image of the whole threefold universe."—Trans.]

107 *Elenchos*, VIII, 12, 5. [Cf. *Aion*, pars. 340ff.—Editors.]

108 Ibid., VIII, 12, 2.

109 Cf. the alchemical dictum: "Seminate aurum in terram albam foliatam" (Sow the gold in white foliated earth).

110 Cf. my remarks on the "uniting symbol" in *Psychological Types*, ch. V, sections 3 and 5.

7. *Patterns of Behaviour and Archetypes*

397   We have stated that the lower reaches of the psyche begin where the function emancipates itself from the compulsive force of instinct and becomes amenable to the will, and we have defined the will as disposable energy. But that, as said, presupposes a disposing subject, capable of judgment and endowed with consciousness. In this way we arrived at the position of proving, as it were, the very thing that we started by rejecting, namely the identification of psyche with consciousness. This dilemma resolves itself once we realize how very relative consciousness is, since its contents are conscious and unconscious at the same time, i.e., conscious under one aspect and unconscious under another. As is the way of paradoxes, this statement is not immediately comprehensible.[111] We must, however, accustom ourselves to the thought that conscious and unconscious have no clear demarcations, the one beginning where the other leaves off. It is rather the case that the psyche is a conscious-unconscious whole. As to the no man's land which I have called the "personal unconscious," it is fairly easy to prove that its contents correspond exactly to our definition of the psychic. But—as we define "psychic"—is there a psychic unconscious that is not a "fringe of consciousness" and not personal?

398   I have already mentioned that Freud established the existence of archaic vestiges and primitive modes of functioning in the unconscious. Subsequent investigations have confirmed this result and brought together a wealth of observational material. In view of the structure of the body, it would be astonishing if the psyche were the only biological phenomenon not to show clear traces of its evolutionary history, and it is altogether probable that these marks are closely connected with the instinctual base. Instinct and the archaic mode meet in the bio-

111 Freud also arrived at similar paradoxical conclusions. Thus, in his article "The Unconscious" (p. 177): he says: "An instinct can never become an object of consciousness—only the idea that represents the instinct can. *Even in the unconscious, moreover, an instinct cannot be represented otherwise than by an idea.*" (My italics.) As in my above account we were left asking, "Who is the subject of the unconscious will?" so we must ask here, "Exactly *who* has the idea of the instinct in the unconscious state?" For "unconscious" ideation is a *contradictio in adjecto*.

logical conception of the "pattern of behaviour." There are, in fact, no amorphous instincts, as every instinct bears in itself the pattern of its situation. Always it fulfils an image, and the image has fixed qualities. The instinct of the leaf-cutting ant fulfils the image of ant, tree, leaf, cutting, transport, and the little ant-garden of fungi.[112] If any one of these conditions is lacking, the instinct does not function, because it cannot exist without its total pattern, without its image. Such an image is an *a priori* type. It is inborn in the ant prior to any activity, for there can be no activity at all unless an instinct of corresponding pattern initiates and makes it possible. This schema holds true of all instincts and is found in identical form in all individuals of the same species. The same is true also of man: he has in him these *a priori* instinct-types which provide the occasion and the pattern for his activities, in so far as he functions instinctively. As a biological being he has no choice but to act in a specifically human way and fulfil his pattern of behaviour. This sets narrow limits to his possible range of volition, the more narrow the more primitive he is, and the more his consciousness is dependent upon the instinctual sphere. Although from one point of view it is quite correct to speak of the pattern of behaviour as a still-existing archaic vestige, as Nietzsche did in respect of the function of dreams, such an attitude does scant justice to the biological and psychological meaning of these types. They are not just relics or vestiges of earlier modes of functioning; they are the ever-present and biologically necessary regulators of the instinctual sphere, whose range of action covers the whole realm of the psyche and only loses its absoluteness when limited by the relative freedom of the will. We may say that the image represents the *meaning* of the instinct.

399   Although the existence of an instinctual pattern in human biology is probable, it seems very difficult to prove the existence of distinct types empirically. For the organ with which we might apprehend them—consciousness—is not only itself a transformation of the original instinctual image, but also its transformer. It is therefore not surprising that the human mind finds it impossible to specify precise types for man similar to those we know in the animal kingdom. I must confess that I can see no

112 For details see C. Lloyd Morgan, *Habit and Instinct.*

direct way to solve this problem. And yet I have succeeded, or so I believe, in finding at least an indirect way of approach to the instinctual image.

400   In what follows, I would like to give a brief description of how this discovery took place. I had often observed patients whose dreams pointed to a rich store of fantasy-material. Equally, from the patients themselves, I got the impression that they were stuffed full of fantasies, without their being able to tell me just where the inner pressure lay. I therefore took up a dream-image or an association of the patient's, and, with this as a point of departure, set him the task of elaborating or developing his theme by giving free rein to his fantasy. This, according to individual taste and talent, could be done in any number of ways, dramatic, dialectic, visual, acoustic, or in the form of dancing, painting, drawing, or modelling. The result of this technique was a vast number of complicated designs whose diversity puzzled me for years, until I was able to recognize that in this method I was witnessing the spontaneous manifestation of an unconscious process which was merely assisted by the technical ability of the patient, and to which I later gave the name "individuation process." But, long before this recognition dawned upon me, I had made the discovery that this method often diminished, to a considerable degree, the frequency and intensity of the dreams, thus reducing the inexplicable pressure exerted by the unconscious. In many cases, this brought a large measure of therapeutic success, which encouraged both myself and the patient to press forward despite the baffling nature of the results.[113] I felt bound to insist that they were baffling, if only to stop myself from framing, on the basis of certain theoretical assumptions, interpretations which I felt were not only inadequate but liable to prejudice the ingenuous productions of the patient. The more I suspected these configurations of harbouring a certain purposefulness, the less inclined I was to risk any theories about them. This reticence was not made easy for me, since in many cases I was dealing with patients who needed an intellectual *point d'appui* if they were not to get totally lost in the darkness. I had to try to give provisional interpretations at least, so far as I was able, interspersing them with innumer-

113 Cf. "The Aims of Psychotherapy," pars. 101ff.; and *Two Essays on Analytical Psychology,* pars. 343ff. [Also "The Transcendent Function," pars. 166ff.]

able "perhapses" and "ifs" and "buts" and never stepping beyond the bounds of the picture lying before me. I always took good care to let the interpretation of each image tail off into a question whose answer was left to the free fantasy-activity of the patient.

401   The chaotic assortment of images that at first confronted me reduced itself in the course of the work to certain well-defined themes and formal elements, which repeated themselves in identical or analogous form with the most varied individuals. I mention, as the most salient characteristics, chaotic multiplicity and order; duality; the opposition of light and dark, upper and lower, right and left; the union of opposites in a third; the quaternity (square, cross); rotation (circle, sphere); and finally the centring process and a radial arrangement that usually followed some quaternary system. Triadic formations, apart from the *complexio oppositorum* in a third, were relatively rare and formed notable exceptions which could be explained by special conditions.[114] The centring process is, in my experience, the never-to-be-surpassed climax of the whole development,[115] and is characterized as such by the fact that it brings with it the greatest possible therapeutic effect. The typical features listed above go to the limits of abstraction, yet at the same time they are the simplest expressions of the formative principles here at work. In actual reality, the patterns are infinitely more variegated and far more concrete than this would suggest. Their variety defies description. I can only say that there is probably no motif in any known mythology that does not at some time appear in these configurations. If there was any conscious knowledge of mythological motifs worth mentioning in my patients, it is left far behind by the ingenuities of creative fantasy. In general, my patients had only a minimal knowledge of mythology.

402   These facts show in an unmistakable manner how fantasies guided by unconscious regulators coincide with the records of man's mental activity as known to us from tradition and ethnological research. All the abstract features I have mentioned are in a certain sense conscious: everyone can count up to four and knows what a circle is and a square; but, as formative principles, they are unconscious, and by the same token their psychological

114 The same applies to the pentadic figures.
115 So far as the development can be ascertained from the objective material.

meaning is not conscious either. My most fundamental views and ideas derive from these experiences. First I made the observations, and only then did I hammer out my views. And so it is with the hand that guides the crayon or brush, the foot that executes the dance-step, with the eye and the ear, with the word and the thought: a dark impulse is the ultimate arbiter of the pattern, an unconscious *a priori* precipitates itself into plastic form, and one has no inkling that another person's consciousness is being guided by these same principles at the very point where one feels utterly exposed to the boundless subjective vagaries of chance. Over the whole procedure there seems to reign a dim foreknowledge not only of the pattern but of its meaning.[116] Image and meaning are identical; and as the first takes shape, so the latter becomes clear. Actually, the pattern needs no interpretation: it portrays its own meaning. There are cases where I can let interpretation go as a therapeutic requirement. Scientific knowledge, of course, is another matter. Here we have to elicit from the sum total of our experience certain concepts of the greatest possible general validity, which are not given *a priori*. This particular work entails a translation of the timeless, ever-present operative archetype into the scientific language of the present.

403   These experiences and reflections lead me to believe that there are certain collective unconscious conditions which act as regulators and stimulators of creative fantasy-activity and call forth corresponding formations by availing themselves of the existing conscious material. They behave exactly like the motive forces of dreams, for which reason active imagination, as I have called this method, to some extent takes the place of dreams. The existence of these unconscious regulators—I sometimes refer to them as "dominants" [117] because of their mode of functioning—seemed to me so important that I based upon it my hypothesis of an impersonal collective unconscious. The most remarkable thing about this method, I felt, was that it did not involve a *reductio in primam figuram,* but rather a synthesis—supported by an attitude voluntarily adopted, though for the rest wholly natural—of passive conscious material and unconscious influences, hence a kind of spontaneous amplification of

116 Cf. *Psychology and Alchemy,* par. 329.
117 Cf. *Two Essays on Analytical Psychology,* par. 151.

the archetypes. The images are not to be thought of as a reduction of conscious contents to their simplest denominator, as this would be the direct road to the primordial images which I said previously was unimaginable; they make their appearance only in the course of amplification.

404   On this natural amplification process I also base my method of eliciting the meaning of dreams, for dreams behave in exactly the same way as active imagination; only the support of conscious contents is lacking. To the extent that the archetypes intervene in the shaping of conscious contents by regulating, modifying, and motivating them, they act like the instincts. It is therefore very natural to suppose that these factors are connected with the instincts and to inquire whether the typical situational patterns which these collective form-principles apparently represent are not in the end identical with the instinctual patterns, namely, with the patterns of behaviour. I must admit that up to the present I have not laid hold of any argument that would finally refute this possibility.

405   Before I pursue my reflections further, I must stress one aspect of the archetypes which will be obvious to anybody who has practical experience of these matters. That is, the archetypes have, when they appear, a distinctly numinous character which can only be described as "spiritual," if "magical" is too strong a word. Consequently this phenomenon is of the utmost significance for the psychology of religion. In its effects it is anything but unambiguous. It can be healing or destructive, but never indifferent, provided of course that it has attained a certain degree of clarity.[118] This aspect deserves the epithet "spiritual" above all else. It not infrequently happens that the archetype appears in the form of a *spirit* in dreams or fantasy-products, or even comports itself like a ghost. There is a mystical aura about

118 Occasionally it is associated with synchronistic or parapsychic effects. I mean by synchronicity, as I have explained elsewhere, the not uncommonly observed "coincidence" of subjective and objective happenings, which just cannot be explained causally, at least in the present state of our knowledge. On this premise astrology is based and the methods of the *I Ching*. These observations, like the astrological findings, are not generally accepted, though as we know this has never hurt the facts. I mention these special effects solely for the sake of completeness and solely for the benefit of those readers who have had occasion to convince themselves of the reality of parapsychic phenomena. For a detailed discussion, see the final paper in this volume.

its numinosity, and it has a corresponding effect upon the emotions. It mobilizes philosophical and religious convictions in the very people who deemed themselves miles above any such fits of weakness. Often it drives with unexampled passion and remorseless logic towards its goal and draws the subject under its spell, from which despite the most desperate resistance he is unable, and finally no longer even willing, to break free, because the experience brings with it a depth and fulness of meaning that was unthinkable before. I fully appreciate the resistance that all rooted convictions are bound to put up against psychological discoveries of this kind. With more foreboding than real knowledge, most people feel afraid of the menacing power that lies fettered in each of us, only waiting for the magic word to release it from the spell. This magic word, which always ends in "ism," works most successfully with those who have the least access to their interior selves and have strayed the furthest from their instinctual roots into the truly chaotic world of *collective consciousness*.

406   In spite or perhaps because of its affinity with instinct, the archetype represents the authentic element of spirit, but a spirit which is not to be identified with the human intellect, since it is the latter's *spiritus rector*. The essential content of all mythologies and all religions and all isms is archetypal. The archetype is spirit or pseudo-spirit: what it ultimately proves to be depends on the attitude of the human mind. Archetype and instinct are the most polar opposites imaginable, as can easily be seen when one compares a man who is ruled by his instinctual drives with a man who is seized by the spirit. But, just as between all opposites there obtains so close a bond that no position can be established or even thought of without its corresponding negation, so in this case also "les extrêmes se touchent." They belong together as correspondences, which is not to say that the one is derivable from the other, but that they subsist side by side as reflections in our own minds of the opposition that underlies all psychic energy. Man finds himself simultaneously driven to act and free to reflect. This contrariety in his nature has no moral significance, for instinct is not in itself bad any more than spirit is good. Both can be both. Negative electricity is as good as positive electricity: first and foremost it is electricity. The psychological opposites, too, must be regarded from a scientific

standpoint. True opposites are never incommensurables; if they were they could never unite. All contrariety notwithstanding, they do show a constant propensity to union, and Nicholas of Cusa defined God himself as a *complexio oppositorum.*

07   Opposites are extreme qualities in any state, by virtue of which that state is perceived to be real, for they form a potential. The psyche is made up of processes whose energy springs from the equilibration of all kinds of opposites. The spirit / instinct antithesis is only one of the commonest formulations, but it has the advantage of reducing the greatest number of the most important and most complex psychic processes to a common denominator. So regarded, psychic processes seem to be balances of energy flowing between spirit and instinct, though the question of whether a process is to be described as spiritual or as instinctual remains shrouded in darkness. Such evaluation or interpretation depends entirely upon the standpoint or state of the conscious mind. A poorly developed consciousness, for instance, which because of massed projections is inordinately impressed by concrete or apparently concrete things and states, will naturally see in the instinctual drives the source of all reality. It remains blissfully unaware of the spirituality of such a philosophical surmise, and is convinced that with this opinion it has established the essential instinctuality of all psychic processes. Conversely, a consciousness that finds itself in opposition to the instincts can, in consequence of the enormous influence then exerted by the archetypes, so subordinate instinct to spirit that the most grotesque "spiritual" complications may arise out of what are undoubtedly biological happenings. Here the instinctuality of the fanaticism needed for such an operation is ignored.

08   Psychic processes therefore behave like a scale along which consciousness "slides." At one moment it finds itself in the vicinity of instinct, and falls under its influence; at another, it slides along to the other end where spirit predominates and even assimilates the instinctual processes most opposed to it. These counter-positions, so fruitful of illusion, are by no means symptoms of the abnormal; on the contrary, they form the twin poles of that psychic one-sidedness which is typical of the normal man of today. Naturally this does not manifest itself only in the

spirit / instinct antithesis; it assumes many other forms, as I have shown in my *Psychological Types*.

409   This "sliding" consciousness is thoroughly characteristic of modern man. But the one-sidedness it causes can be removed by what I have called the "realization of the shadow." A less "poetic" and more scientific-looking Greco-Latin neologism could easily have been coined for this operation. In psychology, however, one is to be dissuaded from ventures of this sort, at least when dealing with eminently practical problems. Among these is the "realization of the shadow," the growing awareness of the inferior part of the personality, which should not be twisted into an intellectual activity, for it has far more the meaning of a suffering and a passion that implicate the whole man. The essence of that which has to be realized and assimilated has been expressed so trenchantly and so plastically in poetic language by the word "shadow" that it would be almost presumptuous not to avail oneself of this linguistic heritage. Even the term "inferior part of the personality" is inadequate and misleading, whereas "shadow" presumes nothing that would rigidly fix its content. The "man without a shadow" is statistically the commonest human type, one who imagines he actually *is* only what he cares to know about himself. Unfortunately neither the so-called religious man nor the man of scientific pretensions forms any exception to this rule.

410   Confrontation with an archetype or instinct is an *ethical* problem of the first magnitude, the urgency of which is felt only by people who find themselves faced with the need to assimilate the unconscious and integrate their personalities. This only falls to the lot of the man who realizes that he has a neurosis or that all is not well with his psychic constitution. These are certainly not the majority. The "common man," who is preponderantly a mass man, acts on the principle of realizing nothing, nor does he need to, because for him the only thing that commits mistakes is that vast anonymity conventionally known as "State" or "Society." But once a man knows that he is, or should be, responsible, he feels responsible also for his psychic constitution, the more so the more clearly he sees what he would have to be in order to become healthier, more stable, and more efficient. Once he is on the way to assimilating the unconscious he can be certain that he will escape no difficulty that is an integral part of

his nature. The mass man, on the other hand, has the privilege of being at all times "not guilty" of the social and political catastrophes in which the whole world is engulfed. His final calculation is thrown out accordingly; whereas the other at least has the possibility of finding a spiritual point of vantage, a kingdom that "is not of this world."

411   It would be an unpardonable sin of omission were one to overlook the *feeling-value* of the archetype. This is extremely important both theoretically and therapeutically. As a numinous factor, the archetype determines the nature of the configurational process and the course it will follow, with seeming foreknowledge, or as though it were already in possession of the goal to be circumscribed by the centring process.[119] I would like to make the way in which the archetype functions clear from this simple example. While sojourning in equatorial east Africa, on the southern slopes of Mount Elgon, I found that the natives used to step out of their huts at sunrise, hold their hands before their mouths, and spit or blow into them vigorously. Then they lifted their arms and held their hands with the palms toward the sun. I asked them the meaning of what they did, but nobody could give me an explanation. They had always done it like that, they said, and had learnt it from their parents. The medicine-man, he would know what it meant. So I asked the medicine-man. He knew as little as the others, but assured me that his grandfather had still known. It was just what people did at every sunrise, and at the first phase of the new moon. For these people, as I was able to show, the moment when the sun or the new moon appeared was "mungu," which corresponds to the Melanesian words "mana" or "mulungu" [120] and is translated by the missionaries as "God." Actually the word *adhista* in Elgonyi means sun as well as God, although they deny that the sun is God. Only the moment when it rises is *mungu* or *adhista*. Spittle and breath mean soul-substance. Hence they offer their soul to God, but do not know what they are doing and never have known. They do it, motivated by the same preconscious archetype which the ancient Egyptians, on their monuments, also ascribed to the sun-worshipping dog-headed baboon, albeit in

119 Cf. *Psychology and Alchemy*, Part II, for evidence of this.
120 [*Mulungu* = 'spirit, soul, daemonism, magic, prestige': *Two Essays,* par. 108, and the first paper in this volume, pars. 117, 123f.—EDITORS.]

full knowledge that this ritual gesture was in honour of God. The behaviour of the Elgonyi certainly strikes us as exceedingly primitive, but we forget that the educated Westerner behaves no differently. What the meaning of the Christmas-tree might be our forefathers knew even less than ourselves, and it is only quite recently that we have bothered to find out at all.

412   The archetype is pure, unvitiated nature,[121] and it is nature that causes man to utter words and perform actions whose meaning is unconscious to him, so unconscious that he no longer gives it a thought. A later, more conscious humanity, faced with such meaningful things whose meaning none could declare, hit upon the idea that these must be the last vestiges of a Golden Age, when there were men who knew all things and taught wisdom to the nations. In the degenerate days that followed, these teachings were forgotten and were now only repeated as mindless mechanical gestures. In view of the findings of modern psychology it cannot be doubted that there are preconscious archetypes which were never conscious and can be established only indirectly through their effects upon the conscious contents. There is in my opinion no tenable argument against the hypothesis that all the psychic functions which today seem conscious to us were once unconscious and yet worked as if they *were* conscious. We could also say that all the psychic phenomena to be found in man were already present in the natural unconscious state. To this it might be objected that it would then be far from clear why there is such a thing as consciousness at all. I would, however, remind the reader that, as we have already seen, all unconscious functioning has the automatic character of an instinct, and that the instincts are always coming into collision or, because of their compulsiveness, pursuing their courses unaltered by any influence even under conditions that may positively endanger the life of the individual. As against this, consciousness enables him to adapt in an orderly way and to check the instincts, and consequently it cannot be dispensed with. Man's capacity for consciousness alone makes him man.

413   The achievement of a synthesis of conscious and unconscious contents, and the conscious realization of the archetype's effects upon the conscious contents, represents the climax of a con-

---

[121] "Nature" here means simply that which is, and always was, given.

centrated spiritual and psychic effort, in so far as this is undertaken consciously and of set purpose. That is to say, the synthesis
can also be prepared in advance and brought to a certain point—
James's "bursting point"—unconsciously, whereupon it irrupts
into consciousness of its own volition and confronts the latter
with the formidable task of assimilating the contents that have
burst in upon it, yet without damaging the viability of the two
systems, i.e., of ego-consciousness on the one hand and the
irrupted complex on the other. Classical examples of this process
are Paul's conversion and the Trinity vision of Nicholas of
Flüe.

¹⁴   By means of "active imagination" we are put in a position of
advantage, for we can then make the discovery of the archetype
without sinking back into the instinctual sphere, which would
only lead to blank unconsciousness or, worse still, to some kind
of intellectual substitute for instinct. This means—to employ
once more the simile of the spectrum—that the instinctual image
is to be located not at the red end but at the violet end of the
colour band. The dynamism of instinct is lodged as it were in
the infra-red part of the spectrum, whereas the instinctual image
lies in the ultra-violet part. If we remember our colour symbolism, then, as I have said, red is not such a bad match for
instinct. But for spirit, as might be expected,¹²² blue would be a
better match than violet. Violet is the "mystic" colour, and it
certainly reflects the indubitably "mystic" or paradoxical quality of the archetype in a most satisfactory way. Violet is a com-
pound of blue and red, although in the spectrum it is a colour
in its own right. Now, it is, as it happens, rather more than just
an edifying thought if we feel bound to emphasize that the
archetype is more accurately characterized by violet, for, as well
as being an image in its own right, it is at the same time a
dynamism which makes itself felt in the numinosity and fascinat-
ing power of the archetypal image. The realization and assimilation of instinct never take place at the red end, i.e., by absorption
into the instinctual sphere, but only through integration of the
image which signifies and at the same time evokes the instinct,
although in a form quite different from the one we meet on the

¹²² This expectation is based on the experience that blue, the colour of air and
sky, is most readily used for depicting spiritual contents, whereas red, the "warm"
colour, is used for feelings and emotions.

biological level. When Faust remarks to Wagner: "You are conscious only of the single urge / O may you never learn to know the other!" this is a saying that could equally well be applied to instinct in general. It has two aspects: on the one hand it is experienced as physiological dynamism, while on the other hand its multitudinous forms enter into consciousness as images and groups of images, where they develop numinous effects which offer, or appear to offer, the strictest possible contrast to instinct physiologically regarded. For anyone acquainted with religious phenomenology it is an open secret that although physical and spiritual passion are deadly enemies, they are nevertheless brothers-in-arms, for which reason it often needs the merest touch to convert the one into the other. Both are real, and together they form a pair of opposites, which is one of the most fruitful sources of psychic energy. There is no point in deriving one from the other in order to give primacy to one of them. Even if we know only one at first, and do not notice the other until much later, that does not prove that the other was not there all the time. Hot cannot be derived from cold, nor high from low. An opposition either exists in its binary form or it does not exist at all, and a being without opposites is completely unthinkable, as it would be impossible to establish its existence.

415   Absorption into the instinctual sphere, therefore, does not and cannot lead to conscious realization and assimilation of instinct, because consciousness struggles in a regular panic against being swallowed up in the primitivity and unconsciousness of sheer instinctuality. This fear is the eternal burden of the hero-myth and the theme of countless taboos. The closer one comes to the instinct-world, the more violent is the urge to shy away from it and to rescue the light of consciousness from the murks of the sultry abyss. Psychologically, however, the archetype as an image of instinct is a spiritual goal toward which the whole nature of man strives; it is the sea to which all rivers wend their way, the prize which the hero wrests from the fight with the dragon.

416   Because the archetype is a formative principle of instinctual power, its blue is contaminated with red: it appears to be violet, or again, we could interpret the simile as an apocatastasis of instinct raised to a higher frequency, just as we could easily

derive instinct from a latent (i.e., transcendent) archetype that manifests itself on a longer wave-length.[123] Although it can admittedly be no more than an analogy, I nevertheless feel tempted to recommend this violet image to my reader as an illustrative hint of the archetype's affinity with its own opposite. The creative fantasy of the alchemists sought to express this abstruse secret of nature by means of another, no less concrete, symbol: the Uroboros, or tail-eating serpent.

17   I do not want to work this simile to death, but, as the reader will understand, one is always delighted, when discussing difficult problems, to find support in a helpful analogy. In addition this simile helps to throw light on a question we have not yet asked ourselves, much less answered, the question regarding the *nature* of the archetype. The archetypal representations (images and ideas) mediated to us by the unconscious should not be confused with the archetype as such. They are very varied structures which all point back to one essentially "irrepresentable" basic form. The latter is characterized by certain formal elements and by certain fundamental meanings, although these can be grasped only approximately. The archetype as such is a psychoid factor that belongs, as it were, to the invisible, ultraviolet end of the psychic spectrum. It does not appear, in itself, to be capable of reaching consciousness. I venture this hypothesis because everything archetypal which is perceived by consciousness seems to represent a set of variations on a ground theme. One is most impressed by this act when one studies the endless variations of the mandala motif. This is a relatively simple ground form whose meaning can be said to be "central." But although it looks like the structure of a centre, it is still uncertain whether within that structure the centre or the periphery, division or non-division, is the more accentuated. Since other archetypes give rise to similar doubts, it seems to me probable that the real nature of the archetype is not capable of being made conscious, that it is transcendent, on which account I call it psychoid. Moreover every archetype, when represented to the mind, is already conscious and therefore differs to an indeterminable extent from that which caused the representation. As

123 Sir James Jeans (*Physics and Philosophy*, p. 193) points out that the shadows on the wall of Plato's cave are just as real as the invisible figures that cast them and whose existence can only be inferred mathematically.

Theodor Lipps has stressed, the nature of the psychic is unconscious. Anything conscious is part of the phenomenal world which—so modern physics teaches—does not supply explanations of the kind that objective reality requires. Objective reality requires a mathematical model, and experience shows that this is based on invisible and irrepresentable factors. Psychology cannot evade the universal validity of this fact, the less so as the observing psyche is already included in any formulation of objective reality. Nor can psychological theory be formulated mathematically, because we have no measuring rod with which to measure psychic quantities. We have to rely solely upon qualities, that is, upon perceptible phenomena. Consequently psychology is incapacitated from making any valid statement about unconscious states, or to put it another way, there is no hope that the validity of any statement about unconscious states or processes will ever be verified scientifically. Whatever we say about the archetypes, they remain visualizations or concretizations which pertain to the field of consciousness. But—we cannot speak about archetypes in any other way. We must, however, constantly bear in mind that what we mean by "archetype" is in itself irrepresentable, but has effects which make visualizations of it possible, namely, the archetypal images and ideas. We meet with a similar situation in physics: there the smallest particles are themselves irrepresentable but have effects from the nature of which we can build up a model. The archetypal image, the motif or mythologem, is a construction of this kind. When the existence of two or more irrepresentables is assumed, there is always the possibility—which we tend to overlook—that it may not be a question of two or more factors but of one only. The identity or non-identity of two irrepresentable quantities is something that cannot be proved. If on the basis of its observations psychology assumes the existence of certain irrepresentable psychoid factors, it is doing the same thing in principle as physics does when the physicist constructs an atomic model. And it is not only psychology that suffers from the misfortune of having to give its object, the unconscious, a name that has often been criticized because it is merely negative; the same thing happened in physics, since it could not avoid using the ancient term "atom" (meaning "indivisible") for the smallest particle of matter. Just as the atom is not indivisible, so, as we shall see, the unconscious is not merely unconscious. And just as physics in its psychological aspect can do no more than establish the existence of an observer without being able to assert anything about the nature of that observer, so psychology can only indicate the relation of psyche to matter without being able to make out the least thing about its nature.

8   Since psyche and matter are contained in one and the same world, and moreover are in continuous contact with one another and ultimately rest on irrepresentable, transcendental factors, it is not only possible but fairly probable, even, that psyche and matter are two different aspects of one and the same thing. The synchronicity phenomena point, it seems to me, in this direction, for they show that the nonpsychic can behave like the psychic, and vice versa, without there being any causal connection between them. Our present knowledge does not allow us to do much more than compare the relation of the psychic to the material world with two cones, whose apices, meeting in a point without extension—a real zero-point—touch and do not touch.

9   In my previous writings I have always treated archetypal phenomena as psychic, because the material to be expounded or investigated was concerned solely with ideas and images. The psychoid nature of the archetype, as put forward here, does not contradict these earlier formulations; it only means a further degree of conceptual differentiation, which became inevitable as soon as I saw myself obliged to undertake a more general analysis of the nature of the psyche and to clarify the empirical concepts concerning it, and their relation to one another.

0   Just as the "psychic infra-red," the biological instinctual psyche, gradually passes over into the physiology of the organism and thus merges with its chemical and physical conditions, so the "psychic ultra-violet," the archetype, describes a field which exhibits none of the peculiarities of the physiological and yet, in the last analysis, can no longer be regarded as psychic, although it manifests itself psychically. But physiological processes behave in the same way, without on that account being declared psychic. Although there is no form of existence that is not mediated to us psychically and only psychically, it would hardly do to say that everything is merely psychic. We must apply this argument logically to the archetypes as well. Since their essential being is unconscious to us, and still they are

experienced as spontaneous agencies, there is probably no alternative now but to describe their nature, in accordance with their chiefest effect, as "spirit," in the sense which I attempted to make plain in my paper "The Phenomenology of the Spirit in Fairytales." If so, the position of the archetype would be located beyond the psychic sphere, analogous to the position of physiological instinct, which is immediately rooted in the stuff of the organism and, with its psychoid nature, forms the bridge to matter in general. In archetypal conceptions and instinctual perceptions, spirit and matter confront one another on the psychic plane. Matter and spirit both appear in the psychic realm as distinctive qualities of conscious contents. The ultimate nature of both is transcendental, that is, irrepresentable, since the psyche and its contents are the only reality which is given to us *without a medium*.

8. *General Considerations and Prospects*

421   The problems of analytical psychology, as I have tried to outline them here, led to conclusions that astonished even me. I fancied I was working along the best scientific lines, establishing facts, observing, classifying, describing causal and functional relations, only to discover in the end that I had involved myself in a net of reflections which extend far beyond natural science and ramify into the fields of philosophy, theology, comparative religion, and the humane sciences in general. This transgression, as inevitable as it was suspect, has caused me no little worry. Quite apart from my personal incompetence in these fields, it seemed to me that my reflections were suspect also in principle, because I am profoundly convinced that the "personal equation" has a telling effect upon the results of psychological observation. The tragic thing is that psychology has no self-consistent mathematics at its disposal, but only a calculus of subjective prejudices. Also, it lacks the immense advantage of an Archimedean point such as physics enjoys. The latter observes the physical world from the psychic standpoint and can translate it into psychic terms. The psyche, on the other hand, observes itself and can only translate the psychic back into the psychic. Were physics in this position, it could do nothing except leave the physical process to its own devices, because in that way

it would be most plainly itself. There is no medium for psychology to reflect itself in: it can only portray itself in itself, and describe itself. That, logically, is also the principle of my own method: it is, at bottom, a purely experiential process in which hit and miss, interpretation and error, theory and speculation, doctor and patient, form a *symptosis* (σύμπτωσις) or a *symptoma* (σύμπτωμα)—a coming together—and at the same time are symptoms of a certain process or run of events. What I am describing, therefore, is basically no more than an outline of psychic happenings which exhibit a certain statistical frequency. We have not, scientifically speaking, removed ourselves to a plane in any way "above" the psychic process, nor have we translated it into another medium. Physics, on the other hand, is in a position to detonate mathematical formulae—the product of pure psychic activity—and kill seventy-eight thousand persons at one blow.

2   This literally "devastating" argument is calculated to reduce psychology to silence. But we can, in all modesty, point out that mathematical thinking is also a psychic function, thanks to which matter can be organized in such a way as to burst asunder the mighty forces that bind the atoms together—which it would never occur to them to do in the natural course of things, at least not upon this earth. The psyche is a disturber of the natural laws of the cosmos, and should we ever succeed in doing something to Mars with the aid of atomic fission, this too will have been brought to pass by the psyche.

3   The psyche is the world's pivot: not only is it the one great condition for the existence of a world at all, it is also an intervention in the existing natural order, and no one can say with certainty where this intervention will finally end. It is hardly necessary to stress the dignity of the psyche as an object of natural science. With all the more urgency, then, we must emphasize that the smallest alteration in the psychic factor, if it be an alteration of principle, is of the utmost significance as regards our knowledge of the world and the picture we make of it. The integration of unconscious contents into consciousness, which is the main endeavour of analytical psychology, is just such an alteration of principle, in that it does away with the sovereignty of the subjective ego-consciousness and confronts it with unconscious collective contents. Accordingly ego-consciousness seems to be dependent on two factors: firstly, on the

conditions of the collective, i.e., the social, consciousness; and secondly, on the archetypes, or dominants, of the collective unconscious. The latter fall phenomenologically into two categories: instinctual and archetypal. The first includes the natural impulses, the second the dominants that emerge into consciousness as universal ideas. Between the contents of collective consciousness, which purport to be generally accepted truths, and those of the collective unconscious there is so pronounced a contrast that the latter are rejected as totally irrational, not to say meaningless, and are most unjustifiably excluded from the scientific purview as though they did not exist. However, psychic phenomena of this kind exist with a vengeance, and if they appear nonsensical to us, that only proves that we do not understand them. Once their existence is recognized they can no longer be banished from our world-picture, even though the prevailing conscious *Weltanschauung* proves to be incapable of grasping the phenomena in question. A conscientious study of these phenomena quickly reveals their uncommon significance, and we can hardly avoid the conclusion that between collective consciousness and the collective unconscious there is an almost unbridgeable gulf over which the subject finds himself suspended.

424   As a rule, collective consciousness wins hands down with its "reasonable" generalities that cause the average intelligence no difficulty whatever. It still believes in the necessary connection of cause and effect and has scarcely taken note of the fact that causality has become relative. The shortest distance between two points is still, for it, a straight line, although physics has to reckon with innumerable shortest distances, which strikes the educated Philistine of today as exquisitely absurd. Nevertheless the impressive explosion at Hiroshima has induced an awestruck respect for even the most abstruse alembications of modern physics. The explosion which we recently had occasion to witness in Europe, though far more terrible in its repercussions, was recognized as an unmitigated psychic disaster only by the few. Rather than do this, people prefer the most preposterous political and economic theories, which are about as useful as explaining the Hiroshima explosion as the chance hit of a large meteorite.

5   If the subjective consciousness prefers the ideas and opinions
of collective consciousness and identifies with them, then the
contents of the collective unconscious are repressed. The repression has typical consequences: the energy-charge of the repressed
contents adds itself, in some measure,[124] to that of the repressing
factor, whose effectiveness is increased accordingly. The higher
its charge mounts, the more the repressive attitude acquires a
fanatical character and the nearer it comes to conversion into its
opposite, i.e., an enantiodromia. And the more highly charged
the collective consciousness, the more the ego forfeits its practical importance. It is, as it were, absorbed by the opinions and
tendencies of collective consciousness, and the result of that is
the mass man, the ever-ready victim of some wretched "ism."
The ego keeps its integrity only if it does not identify with one
of the opposites, and if it understands how to hold the balance
between them. This is possible only if it remains conscious of
both at once. However, the necessary insight is made exceedingly difficult not by one's social and political leaders alone, but
also by one's religious mentors. They all want decision in favour
of one thing, and therefore the utter identification of the individual with a necessarily one-sided "truth." Even if it were a
question of some great truth, identification with it would still
be a catastrophe, as it arrests all further spiritual development.
Instead of knowledge one then has only belief, and sometimes
that is more convenient and therefore more attractive.

6   If, on the other hand, the content of the collective unconscious is realized, if the existence and efficacy of archetypal
representations are acknowledged, then a violent conflict usually
breaks out between what Fechner has called the "day-time and
the night-time view." Medieval man (and modern man too, in
so far as he has kept the attitude of the past) lived fully conscious of the discord between worldliness, which was subject to

---

[124] It is very probable that the archetypes, as instincts, possess a specific energy
which cannot be taken away from them in the long run. The energy peculiar to
the archetype is normally not sufficient to raise it into consciousness. For this it
needs a definite quantum of energy flowing into the unconscious from consciousness, whether because consciousness is not using this energy or because the archetype attracts it to itself. The archetype can be deprived of its supplementary
charge, but not of its specific energy.

the *princeps huius mundi* (St. John 12 : 31 and 16 : 11 [125]), and the will of God. For centuries this contradiction was demonstrated before his very eyes by the struggle between imperial and papal power. On the moral plane the conflict swelled to the everlasting cosmic tug of war between good and evil in which man was implicated on account of original sin. The medieval man had not yet fallen such a helpless victim to worldliness as the contemporary mass man, for, to offset the notorious and, so to speak, tangible powers of this world, he still acknowledged the equally influential metaphysical potencies which demanded to be taken into account. Although in one respect he was politically and socially unfree and without rights—e.g., as a serf—and also found himself in the extremely disagreeable situation of being tyrannized over by black superstition, he was at least biologically nearer to that unconscious wholeness which primitive man enjoys in even larger measure, and the wild animal possesses to perfection. Looked at from the standpoint of modern consciousness, the position of medieval man seems as deplorable as it is in need of improvement. But the much needed broadening of the mind by science has only replaced medieval one-sidedness—namely, that age-old unconsciousness which once predominated and has gradually become defunctive—by a new one-sidedness, the overvaluation of "scientifically" attested views. These each and all relate to knowledge of the external object and in a chronically one-sided way, so that nowadays the backwardness of psychic development in general and of self-knowledge in particular has become one of the most pressing contemporary problems. As a result of the prevailing one-sidedness, and in spite of the terrifying optical demonstration of an unconscious that has become alienated from the conscious, there are still vast numbers of people who are the blind and helpless victims of these conflicts, and who apply their scientific scrupulosity only to external objects, never to their own psychic condition. Yet the psychic facts are as much in need of objective scrutiny and acknowledgment. There are objective psychic factors which are every bit as important as radios and automobiles. Ultimately everything (particularly in the case of the atom-

125 Although both passages hint that the devil was cast out during the life-time of Jesus, in the Apocalypse the business of rendering him harmless is deferred until Doomsday (Rev. 20 : 2ff.).

bomb) depends on the uses to which these factors are put, and that is always conditioned by one's state of mind. The current "isms" are the most serious threat in this respect, because they are nothing but dangerous identifications of the subjective with the collective consciousness. Such an identity infallibly produces a mass psyche with its irresistible urge to catastrophe. Subjective consciousness must, in order to escape this doom, avoid identification with collective consciousness by recognizing its shadow as well as the existence and the importance of the archetypes. These latter are an effective defence against the brute force of collective consciousness and the mass psyche that goes with it. In point of effectiveness, the religious outlook of medieval man corresponds roughly to the attitude induced in the ego by the integration of unconscious contents, with the difference that in the latter case susceptibility to environmental influences and unconsciousness are replaced by scientific objectivity and conscious knowledge. But so far as religion, for the contemporary consciousness, still means, if anything, a creed, and hence a collectively accepted system of religious statements neatly codified as dogmatic precepts, it has closer affinities with collective consciousness even though its symbols express the once-operative archetypes. So long as the communal consciousness presided over by the Church is objectively present, the psyche, as said, continues to enjoy a certain equilibrium. At all events, it constitutes a sufficiently effective defence against inflation of the ego. But once Mother Church and her motherly Eros fall into abeyance, the individual is at the mercy of any passing collectivism and the attendant mass psyche. He succumbs to social or national inflation, and the tragedy is that he does so with the same psychic attitude which had once bound him to a church.

27   But if he is independent enough to recognize the bigotedness of the social "ism," he may then be threatened with subjective inflation, for usually he is not capable of seeing that religious ideas do not, in psychological reality, rest solely upon tradition and faith, but originate with the archetypes, the "careful consideration" of which—*religere!*—constitutes the essence of religion. The archetypes are continuously present and active; as such they need no believing in, but only an intuition of their meaning and a certain sapient awe, a δεισιδαιμονία, which never

131

loses sight of their import. A consciousness sharpened by experience knows the catastrophic consequences that disregard of this entails for the individual as well as for society. Just as the archetype is partly a spiritual factor, and partly like a hidden meaning immanent in the instincts, so the spirit, as I have shown,[126] is two-faced and paradoxical: a great help and an equally great danger.[127] It seems as if man were destined to play a decisive role in solving this uncertainty, and to solve it moreover by virtue of his consciousness, which once started up like a light in the murk of the primeval world. Nowhere do we know for sure about these matters, but least of all where "isms" flourish, for they are only a sophisticated substitute for the lost link with psychic reality. The mass psyche that infallibly results destroys the meaning of the individual and of culture generally.

428   From this it is clear that the psyche not only disturbs the natural order but, if it loses its balance, actually destroys its own creation. Therefore the careful consideration of psychic factors is of importance in restoring not merely the individual's balance, but society's as well, otherwise the destructive tendencies easily gain the upper hand. In the same way that the atom-bomb is an unparalleled means of physical mass destruction, so the misguided development of the soul must lead to psychic mass destruction. The present situation is so sinister that one cannot suppress the suspicion that the Creator is planning another deluge that will finally exterminate the existing race of men. But if anyone imagines that a healthy belief in the existence of archetypes can be inculcated from outside, he is as simple as the people who want to outlaw war or the atom-bomb. Such measures remind one of the bishop who excommunicated the cockchafers for their unseemly proliferation. Change of consciousness begins at home; it is an age-long process that depends entirely on how far the psyche's capacity for development extends. All we know at present is that there are single individuals who are capable of developing. How great their total number is we do not know, just as we do not know what the suggestive power of an extended consciousness may be, or what influence it may

126 Cf. "The Phenomenology of the Spirit in Fairytales."
127 Aptly expressed in the logion cited by Origen (*Homiliae in Jeremiam*, XX, 3): "He who is near unto me is near unto the fire. He who is far from me is far from the kingdom." This "unclaimed saying of the Master" refers to Isaiah 33 : 14.

have upon the world at large. Effects of this kind never depend on the reasonableness of an idea, but far more on the question (which can only be answered *ex effectu*): is the time ripe for change, or not?

*

29   As I have said, the psychology of complex phenomena finds itself in an uncomfortable situation compared with the other natural sciences because it lacks a base outside its object. It can only translate itself back into its own language, or fashion itself in its own image. The more it extends its field of research and the more complicated its objects become, the more it feels the lack of a point which is distinct from those objects. And once the complexity has reached that of the empirical man, his psychology inevitably merges with the psychic process itself. It can no longer be distinguished from the latter, and so turns into it. But the effect of this is that the process attains to consciousness. In this way, psychology actualizes the unconscious urge to consciousness. It is, in fact, the coming to consciousness of the psychic process, but it is not, in the deeper sense, an explanation of this process, for no explanation of the psychic can be anything other than the living process of the psyche itself. Psychology is doomed to cancel itself out as a science and therein precisely it reaches its scientific goal. Every other science has so to speak an outside; not so psychology, whose object is the inside subject of all science.

130   Psychology therefore culminates of necessity in a developmental process which is peculiar to the psyche and consists in integrating the unconscious contents into consciousness. This means that the psychic human being becomes a whole, and becoming whole has remarkable effects on ego-consciousness which are extremely difficult to describe. I doubt my ability to give a proper account of the change that comes over the subject under the influence of the individuation process; it is a relatively rare occurrence, which is experienced only by those who have gone through the wearisome but, if the unconscious is to be integrated, indispensable business of coming to terms with the unconscious components of the personality. Once these unconscious components are made conscious, it results not only in

their assimilation to the already existing ego-personality, but in a transformation of the latter. The main difficulty is to describe the manner of this transformation. Generally speaking the ego is a hard-and-fast complex which, because tied to consciousness and its continuity, cannot easily be altered, and should not be altered unless one wants to bring on pathological disturbances. The closest analogies to an alteration of the ego are to be found in the field of psychopathology, where we meet not only with neurotic dissociations but also with the schizophrenic fragmentation, or even dissolution, of the ego. In this field, too, we can observe pathological attempts at integration— if such an expression be permitted. These consist in more or less violent irruptions of unconscious contents into consciousness, the ego proving itself incapable of assimilating the intruders. But if the structure of the ego-complex is strong enough to withstand their assault without having its framework fatally dislocated, then assimilation can take place. In that event there is an alteration of the ego as well as of the unconscious contents. Although it is able to preserve its structure, the ego is ousted from its central and dominating position and thus finds itself in the role of a passive observer who lacks the power to assert his will under all circumstances, not so much because it has been weakened in any way, as because certain considerations give it pause. That is, the ego cannot help discovering that the afflux of unconscious contents has vitalized the personality, enriched it and created a figure that somehow dwarfs the ego in scope and intensity. This experience paralyzes an over-egocentric will and convinces the ego that in spite of all difficulties it is better to be taken down a peg than to get involved in a hopeless struggle in which one is invariably handed the dirty end of the stick. In this way the will, as disposable energy, gradually subordinates itself to the stronger factor, namely to the new totality-figure I call the *self*. Naturally, in these circumstances there is the greatest temptation simply to follow the power-instinct and to identify the ego with the self outright, in order to keep up the illusion of the ego's mastery. In other cases the ego proves too weak to offer the necessary resistance to the influx of unconscious contents and is thereupon assimilated by the unconscious, which produces a blurring or darkening of ego-consciousness and its identification with a preconscious wholeness.[128] Both these developments make the realization of the self impossible, and at the same time are fatal to the maintenance of ego-consciousness. They amount, therefore, to pathological effects. The psychic phenomena recently observable in Germany fall into this category. It is abundantly clear that such an *abaissement du niveau mental,* i.e., the overpowering of the ego by unconscious contents and the consequent identification with a preconscious wholeness, possesses a prodigious psychic virulence, or power of contagion, and is capable of the most disastrous results. Developments of this kind should, therefore, be watched very carefully; they require the closest control. I would recommend anyone who feels himself threatened by such tendencies to hang a picture of St. Christopher on the wall and to meditate upon it. For the self has a functional meaning only when it can act compensatorily to ego-consciousness. If the ego is dissolved in identification with the self, it gives rise to a sort of nebulous superman with a puffed-up ego and a deflated self. Such a personage, however saviourlike or baleful his demeanour, lacks the *scintilla,* the soul-spark, the little wisp of divine light that never burns more brightly than when it has to struggle against the invading darkness. What would the rainbow be were it not limned against the lowering cloud?

431   This simile is intended to remind the reader that pathological analogies of the individuation process are not the only ones. There are spiritual monuments of quite another kind, and they are positive illustrations of our process. Above all I would mention the *koans* of Zen Buddhism, those sublime paradoxes that light up, as with a flash of lightning, the inscrutable interrelations between ego and self. In very different language, St. John of the Cross has made the same problem more readily accessible to the Westerner in his account of the "dark night of the soul." That we find it needful to draw analogies from psychopathology and from both Eastern and Western mysticism is only to be expected: the individuation process is, psychically, a border-line

128 Conscious wholeness consists in a successful union of ego and self, so that both preserve their intrinsic qualities. If, instead of this union, the ego is overpowered by the self, then the self too does not attain the form it ought to have, but remains fixed on a primitive level and can express itself only through archaic symbols.

phenomenon which needs special conditions in order to become conscious. Perhaps it is the first step along a path of development to be trodden by the men of the future—a path which, for the time being, has taken a pathological turn and landed Europe in catastrophe.

432   To one familiar with our psychology, it may seem a waste of time to keep harping on the long-established difference between becoming conscious and the coming-to-be of the self (individuation). But again and again I note that the individuation process is confused with the coming of the ego into consciousness and that the ego is in consequence identified with the self, which naturally produces a hopeless conceptual muddle. Individuation is then nothing but ego-centredness and autoeroticism. But the self comprises infinitely more than a mere ego, as the symbolism has shown from of old. It is as much one's self, and all other selves, as the ego. Individuation does not shut one out from the world, but gathers the world to oneself.

433   With this I would like to bring my exposition to an end. I have tried to sketch out the development and basic problems of our psychology and to communicate the quintessence, the very spirit, of this science. In view of the unusual difficulties of my theme, the reader may pardon the undue demands I have made upon his good-will and attention. Fundamental discussions are among the things that mould a science into shape, but they are seldom entertaining.

Supplement

434   As the points of view that have to be considered in elucidating the unconscious are often misunderstood, I would like, in connection with the foregoing discussions of principle, to examine at least two of the main prejudices somewhat more closely.

435   What above all stultifies understanding is the arrant assumption that "archetype" means an inborn idea. No biologist would ever dream of assuming that each individual acquires his general mode of behaviour afresh each time. It is much more probable that the young weaver-bird builds his characteristic nest because he is a weaver-bird and not a rabbit. Similarly, it is more probable that man is born with a specifically human mode

of behaviour and not with that of a hippopotamus or with none at all. Integral to his characteristic behaviour is his psychic phenomenology, which differs from that of a bird or quadruped. Archetypes are typical forms of behaviour which, once they become conscious, naturally present themselves *as ideas and images,* like everything else that becomes a content of consciousness. Because it is a question of characteristically human modes, it is hardly to be wondered at that we can find psychic forms in the individual which occur not only at the antipodes but also in other epochs with which archaeology provides the only link.

36   Now if we wish to prove that a certain psychic form is not a unique but a typical occurrence, this can be done only if I myself testify that, having taken the necessary precautions, I have observed the same thing in different individuals. Then other observers, too, must confirm that they have made the same or similar observations. Finally we have to establish that the same or similar phenomena can be shown to occur in the folklore of other peoples and races and in the texts that have come down to us from earlier centuries and epochs. My method and whole outlook, therefore, begin with individual psychic facts which not I alone have established, but other observers as well. The material brought forward—folkloristic, mythological, or historical—serves in the first place to demonstrate the uniformity of psychic events in time and space. But, since the meaning and substance of the typical individual forms are of the utmost importance in practice, and knowledge of them plays a considerable role in each individual case, it is inevitable that the mythologem and its content will also be drawn into the limelight. This is not to say that the purpose of the investigation is to interpret the mythologem. But, precisely in this connection, a widespread prejudice reigns that the psychology of unconscious processes is a sort of *philosophy* designed to explain mythologems. This unfortunately rather common prejudice assiduously overlooks the crucial point, namely, that our psychology starts with observable facts and not with philosophical speculations. If, for instance, we study the mandala structures that are always cropping up in dreams and fantasies, ill-considered criticism might raise, and indeed has raised, the objection that we are reading Indian or Chinese philosophy into the psyche. But in reality all we have done is to compare individual

psychic occurrences with obviously related collective phenomena. The introspective trend of Eastern philosophy has brought
to light material which all introspective attitudes bring to light
all over the world, at all times and places. The great snag so far
as the critic is concerned is that he has no personal experience
of the facts in question, any more than he has of the state of
mind of a lama engaged in "constructing" a mandala. These
two prejudices render any access to modern psychology impossible for not a few heads with scientific pretensions. There are
in addition many other stumbling-blocks that cannot be overcome by reason. We shall therefore refrain from discussing
them.

437   Inability to understand, or the ignorance of the public, cannot however prevent the scientist from employing certain
calculations of probability, of whose treacherous nature he is
sufficiently well informed. We are fully aware that we have no
more knowledge of the various states and processes of the unconscious as such than the physicist has of the process underlying
physical phenomena. Of what lies beyond the phenomenal
world we can have absolutely no idea, for there is no idea that
could have any other source than the phenomenal world. If we
are to engage in fundamental reflections about the nature of the
psychic, we need an Archimedean point which alone makes a
judgment possible. This can only be the nonpsychic, for, as a
living phenomenon, the psychic lies embedded in something
that appears to be of a nonpsychic nature. Although we perceive
the latter as a psychic datum only, there are sufficient reasons
for believing in its objective reality. This reality, so far as it lies
outside our body's limits, is mediated to us chiefly by particles of
light impinging on the retina of the eye. The organization of
these particles produces a picture of the phenomenal world
which depends essentially upon the constitution of the apperceiving psyche on the one hand, and upon that of the light
medium on the other. The apperceiving consciousness has
proved capable of a high degree of development, and constructs
instruments with the help of which our range of seeing and
hearing has been extended by many octaves. Consequently the
postulated reality of the phenomenal world as well as the subjective world of consciousness have undergone an unparalleled
expansion. The existence of this remarkable correlation be-

tween consciousness and the phenomenal world, between subjective perception and objectively real processes, i.e., their
energic effects, requires no further proof.

8   As the phenomenal world is an aggregate of processes of
atomic magnitude, it is naturally of the greatest importance to
find out whether, and if so how, the photons (shall we say)
enable us to gain a definite knowledge of the reality underlying
the mediative energy processes. Experience has shown that light
and matter both behave like separate particles and also like
waves. This paradoxical conclusion obliged us to abandon, on
the plane of atomic magnitudes, a causal description of nature
in the ordinary space-time system, and in its place to set up
invisible fields of probability in multidimensional spaces, which
do in fact represent the state of our knowledge at present.
Basic to this abstract scheme of explanation is a conception of
reality that takes account of the uncontrollable effects the observer has upon the system observed, the result being that
reality forfeits something of its objective character and that a
subjective element attaches to the physicist's picture of the
world.[129]

9   The application of statistical laws to processes of atomic
magnitude in physics has a noteworthy correspondence in
psychology, so far as psychology investigates the bases of consciousness by pursuing the conscious processes until they lose
themselves in darkness and unintelligibility, and nothing more
can be seen but effects which have an *organizing* influence on
the contents of consciousness.[130] Investigation of these effects

[129] I owe this formulation to the kind help of Professor W. Pauli.

[130] It may interest the reader to hear the opinion of a physicist on this point.
Professor Pauli, who was good enough to glance through the ms. of this supplement, writes: "As a matter of fact the physicist would expect a psychological
correspondence at this point, because the epistemological situation with regard
to the concepts 'conscious' and 'unconscious' seems to offer a pretty close analogy
to the undermentioned 'complementarity' situation in physics. On the one hand
the unconscious can only be inferred indirectly from its (organizing) effects on
conscious contents. On the other hand every 'observation of the unconscious,'
i.e., every conscious realization of unconscious contents, has an uncontrollable
reactive effect on these same contents (which as we know precludes in principle
the possibility of 'exhausting' the unconscious by making it conscious). Thus the
physicist will conclude *per analogiam* that this uncontrollable reactive effect
of the observing subject on the unconscious limits the objective character of the
latter's reality and lends it at the same time a certain subjectivity. Although the

yields the singular fact that they proceed from an unconscious, i.e., objective, reality which behaves at the same time like a subjective one—in other words, like a consciousness. Hence the reality underlying the unconscious effects includes the observing subject and is therefore constituted in a way that we cannot conceive. It is, at one and the same time, absolute subjectivity and universal truth, for in principle it can be shown to be present everywhere, which certainly cannot be said of conscious contents of a personalistic nature. The elusiveness, capriciousness, haziness, and uniqueness that the lay mind always associates with the idea of the psyche applies only to consciousness, and not to the absolute unconscious. The qualitatively rather than quantitatively definable units with which the unconscious works, namely the archetypes, therefore have a nature that *cannot with certainty be designated as psychic.*

440 Although I have been led by purely psychological considerations to doubt the exclusively psychic nature of the archetypes, psychology sees itself obliged to revise its "only psychic" assumptions in the light of the physical findings too. Physics has demonstrated, as plainly as could be wished, that in the realm of atomic magnitudes an observer is postulated in objective reality, and that only on this condition is a satisfactory scheme of explanation possible. This means that a subjective element attaches to the physicist's world picture, and secondly that a connection necessarily exists between the psyche to be explained and the objective space-time continuum. Since the physical continuum is inconceivable it follows that we can form no picture of its

position of the 'cut' between conscious and unconscious is (at least up to a point) left to the free choice of the 'psychological experimenter,' the *existence* of this 'cut' remains an unavoidable necessity. Accordingly, from the standpoint of the psychologist, the 'observed system' would consist not of physical objects only, but would also include the unconscious, while consciousness would be assigned the role of 'observing medium.' It is undeniable that the development of 'microphysics' has brought the way in which nature is described in this science very much closer to that of the newer psychology: but whereas the former, on account of the basic 'complementarity' situation, is faced with the impossibility of eliminating the effects of the observer by determinable correctives, and has therefore to abandon in principle any objective understanding of physical phenomena, the latter can supplement the purely subjective psychology of consciousness by postulating the existence of an unconscious that possesses a large measure of objective reality."

psychic aspect either, which also necessarily exists. Nevertheless, the relative or partial identity of psyche and physical continuum is of the greatest importance theoretically, because it brings with it a tremendous simplification by bridging over the seeming incommensurability between the physical world and the psychic, not of course in any concrete way, but from the physical side by means of mathematical equations, and from the psychological side by means of empirically derived postulates—archetypes—whose content, if any, cannot be represented to the mind. Archetypes, so far as we can observe and experience them at all, manifest themselves only through their ability to *organize* images and ideas, and this is always an unconscious process which cannot be detected until afterwards. By assimilating ideational material whose provenance in the phenomenal world is not to be contested, they become visible and *psychic*. Therefore they are recognized at first only as psychic entities and are conceived as such, with the same right with which we base the physical phenomena of immediate perception on Euclidean space. Only when it comes to explaining psychic phenomena of a minimal degree of clarity are we driven to assume that archetypes must have a nonpsychic aspect. Grounds for such a conclusion are supplied by the phenomena of synchronicity, which are associated with the activity of unconscious operators and have hitherto been regarded, or repudiated, as "telepathy," etc.[131] Scepticism should, however, be levelled only at incorrect theories and not at facts which exist in their own right. No unbiased observer can deny them. Resistance to the recognition of such facts rests principally on the repugnance people feel for an allegedly supernatural faculty tacked on to the psyche, like "clairvoyance." The very diverse and confusing aspects of these phenomena are, so far as I can see at present, completely explicable on the assumption of a psychically relative space-time continuum. As soon as a psychic content crosses the threshold of consciousness, the synchronistic marginal phenomena disappear, time and space resume their accustomed sway, and consciousness is once more isolated in its subjectivity. We have here one of those instances which can best be understood in terms of

131 The physicist Pascual Jordan ("Positivistische Bemerkungen über die parapsychischen Erscheinungen," 14ff.) has already used the idea of relative space to explain telepathic phenomena.

the physicist's idea of "complementarity." When an unconscious content passes over into consciousness its synchronistic manifestation ceases; conversely, synchronistic phenomena can be evoked by putting the subject into an unconscious state (trance). The same relationship of complementarity can be observed just as easily in all those extremely common medical cases in which certain clinical symptoms disappear when the corresponding unconscious contents are made conscious. We also know that a number of psychosomatic phenomena which are otherwise outside the control of the will can be induced by hypnosis, that is, by this same restriction of consciousness. Professor Pauli formulates the physical side of the complementarity relationship here expressed, as follows: "It rests with the free choice of the experimenter (or observer) to decide . . . which insights he will gain and which he will lose; or, to put it in popular language, whether he will measure A and ruin B or ruin A and measure B. It does *not* rest with him, however, to gain only insights and not lose any." This is particularly true of the relation between the physical standpoint and the psychological. Physics determines quantities and their relation to one another; psychology determines qualities without being able to measure quantities. Despite that, both sciences arrive at ideas which come significantly close to one another. The parallelism of psychological and physical explanations has already been pointed out by C. A. Meier in his essay "Moderne Physik—Moderne Psychologie." [132] He says: "Both sciences have, in the course of many years of independent work, amassed observations and systems of thought to match them. Both sciences have come up against certain barriers which . . . display similar basic characteristics. The object to be investigated, and the human investigator with his organs of sense and knowledge and their extensions (measuring instruments and procedures), are indissolubly bound together. That is complementarity in physics as well as in psychology." Between physics and psychology there is in fact "a genuine and authentic relationship of complementarity."

441   Once we can rid ourselves of the highly unscientific pretense that it is merely a question of chance coincidence, we shall see that synchronistic phenomena are not unusual occurrences at

---

[132] *Die kulturelle Bedeutung der komplexen Psychologie*, p. 362.

all, but are relatively common. This fact is in entire agreement with Rhine's "probability-exceeding" results. The psyche is not a chaos made up of random whims and accidents, but is an objective reality to which the investigator can gain access by the methods of natural science. There are indications that psychic processes stand in some sort of energy relation to the physiological substrate. In so far as they are objective events, they can hardly be interpreted as anything but energy processes,[133] or to put it another way: in spite of the nonmeasurability of psychic processes, the perceptible changes effected by the psyche cannot possibly be understood except as a phenomenon of energy. This places the psychologist in a situation which is highly repugnant to the physicist: the psychologist also talks of energy although he has nothing measurable to manipulate, besides which the concept of energy is a strictly defined mathematical quantity which cannot be applied as such to anything psychic. The formula for kinetic energy, $E = \dfrac{mv^2}{2}$, contains the factors m (mass) and v (velocity), and these would appear to be incommensurable with the nature of the empirical psyche. If psychology nevertheless insists on employing its own concept of energy for the purpose of expressing the activity (ἐνέργεια) of the psyche, it is not of course being used as a mathematical formula, but only as its analogy. But note: the analogy is itself an older intuitive idea from which the concept of physical energy originally developed. The latter rests on earlier applications of an ἐνέργεια not mathematically defined, which can be traced back to the primitive or archaic idea of the "extraordinarily potent." This mana concept is not confined to Melanesia, but can also be found in Indonesia and on the east coast of Africa; and it still echoes in the Latin *numen* and, more faintly, in *genius* (e.g., *genius loci*). The use of the term *libido* in the newer medical psychology has surprising affinities with the primitive mana.[134] This archetypal idea is therefore far from being only primitive, but differs from the physicist's conception of energy by the fact that it is essentially qualitative and not quantitative. In psychology the

133 By this I only mean that psychic phenomena have an energic aspect by virtue of which they can be described as "phenomena." I do not mean that the energic aspect embraces or explains the whole of the psyche.
134 Cf. the first paper in this volume.

exact measurement of quantities is replaced by an approximate determination of intensities, for which purpose, in strictest contrast to physics, we enlist the function of *feeling* (valuation). The latter takes the place, in psychology, of concrete measurement in physics. The psychic intensities and their graduated differences point to quantitative processes which are inaccessible to direct observation and measurement. While psychological data are essentially qualitative, they also have a sort of latent physical energy, since psychic phenomena exhibit a certain quantitative aspect. Could these quantities be measured the psyche would be bound to appear as having motion in space, something to which the energy formula would be applicable. Therefore, since mass and energy are of the same nature, mass and velocity would be adequate concepts for characterizing the psyche so far as it has any observable effects in space: in other words, it must have an aspect under which it would appear as mass in motion. If one is unwilling to postulate a pre-established harmony of physical and psychic events, then they can only be in a state of interaction. But the latter hypothesis requires a psyche that touches matter at some point, and, conversely, a matter with a latent psyche, a postulate not so very far removed from certain formulations of modern physics (Eddington, Jeans, and others). In this connection I would remind the reader of the existence of parapsychic phenomena whose reality value can only be appreciated by those who have had occasion to satisfy themselves by personal observation.

442   If these reflections are justified, they must have weighty consequences with regard to the nature of the psyche, since as an objective fact it would then be intimately connected not only with physiological and biological phenomena but with physical events too—and, so it would appear, most intimately of all with those that pertain to the realm of atomic physics. As my remarks may have made clear, we are concerned first and foremost to establish certain analogies, and no more than that; the existence of such analogies does not entitle us to conclude that the connection is already proven. We must, in the present state of our physical and psychological knowledge, be content with the mere resemblance to one another of certain basic reflections. The existing analogies, however, are significant enough in themselves to warrant the prominence we have given them.

BIBLIOGRAPHY

BIBLIOGRAPHY

AGRIPPA VON NETTESHEIM, HEINRICH (HENRICUS) CORNELIUS. *De occulta philosophia libri tres.* Cologne, 1533. For translation, see: *Three Books of Occult Philosophy.* Translated by "J. F." London, 1651. Republished (Book I only) as: *The Occult Philosophy or Magic.* Edited by Willis F. Whitehead. Chicago, 1898.

ARTIS AURIFERAE quam chemiam vocant . . . Basileae [Basel], [1593]. 2 vols.

Contents quoted in this volume:

VOLUME I

   i   Aurora consurgens, quae dicitur Aurea hora [pp. 185–246]

VOLUME II

   ii   Morienus Romanus: Sermo de transmutatione metallica [Liber de compositione Alchemiae] (pp. 7–54).

"Aurora consurgens." See *Artis auriferae, i.*

BASTIAN, ADOLF. *Ethnische Elementargedanken in der Lehre vom Menschen.* Berlin, 1895. 2 parts.

——. *Der Mensch in der Geschichte.* Leipzig, 1860. 3 vols.

BERGER, HANS. *Über die körperlichen Äusserungen psychischer Zustände.* Jena, 1904.

BINSWANGER, LUDWIG. "On the Psycho-galvanic Phenomenon in Association Experiments." In: JUNG, *Studies in Word-Association,* q.v. (pp. 446–530).

BLEULER, EUGEN. *Naturgeschichte der Seele und ihres Bewusstwerdens.* Berlin, 1921.

——. *Die Psychoide als Prinzip der organischen Entwicklung.* Berlin, 1925.

BOLTZMANN, LUDWIG. *Populäre Schriften.* Leipzig, 1905.

BUSEMANN, ADOLF. *Die Einheit der Psychologie.* Stuttgart, 1948.

BUSSE, LUDWIG. *Geist und Körper, Seele und Leib.* Leipzig, 1903.

BUTLER, SAMUEL. *Hudibras.* Edited by A. R. Waller. Cambridge, 1905.

CARPENTER, WILLIAM B. *Principles of Mental Physiology*. London, 1874; 4th edn., 1876.

CHAMBERLAIN, HOUSTON STEWART. *Goethe*. Munich, 1912.

CODRINGTON, ROBERT HENRY. *The Melanesians*. Oxford, 1891.

COOMARASWAMY, ANANDA K. "Rgveda 10.90.1 áty atisthad daśangulám," *Journal of American Oriental Society* (Boston, Mass.), LVI (1946), 145–61.

CRAWLEY, ALFRED ERNEST. *The Idea of the Soul*. London, 1909.

CUMONT, FRANZ. *Textes et monuments figurés relatifs aux mystères de Mithra*. Brussels, 1894–99. 2 vols.

DESSOIR, MAX. *Geschichte der neueren deutschen Psychologie*. 2nd edn., Berlin, 1902. 2 vols.

DORN, GERHARD. See *Theatrum chemicum*, **i–iii.**

DRIESCH, HANS. *Philosophie des Organischen*. Leipzig, 1909. 2 vols. 2nd edn., Leipzig, 1921. 1 vol. For translation, see: *The Science and Philosophy of the Organism*. 2nd edn., London, 1929.

——. *Die "Seele" als elementarer Naturfaktor*. Leipzig, 1903.

EISLER, ROBERT. *Weltenmantel und Himmelszelt*. Munich, 1910. 2 vols.

FECHNER, GUSTAV THEODOR. *Elemente der Psychophysik*. 2nd edn., Leipzig, 1889. 2 vols.

FLOURNOY, THÉODORE. *From India to the Planet Mars*. Translated by D. B. Vermilye. New York and London, 1900. (Orig.: *Des Indes à la Planète Mars; Étude sur un cas de somnambulisme avec glossolalie*. Paris and Geneva, 3rd edn., 1900.)

FRANZ, MARIE-LOUISE VON. "Der Traum des Descartes." In: *Zeitlose Dokumente der Seele*. (Studien aus dem C. G. Jung Institut, 3.) Zurich, 1952.

FREUD, SIGMUND. *Introductory Lectures on Psycho-Analysis*. Translated by Joan Riviere. London, 1922.

——. *Sammlung kleiner Schriften zur Neurosenlehre*. Vienna, 1906–22. 5 vols. (Mostly translated in: *Collected Papers of Sigmund Freud*, Vols. I–IV. London, 1924–25.)

——. "The Unconscious." *Papers on Metapsychology*. In: The Standard Edition of the Complete Psychological Works, 14. Translated by James Strachey et al. London, 1957. (Pp. 159–215.)

FROBENIUS, LEO. *Das Zeitalter des Sonnengottes.* Berlin, 1904.

FUNK, PHILIPP. *Ignatius von Loyola.* (Die Klassiker der Religion, 6.) Berlin, 1913.

GATSCHET, ALBERT SAMUEL. "The Klamath Indians of South-Western Oregon." In: *Contributions to North American Ethnology,* Vol. II. (Miscellaneous Documents of the House of Representatives for the First Session of the 51st Congress, 1889–90; United States Department of the Interior, U.S. Geographical and Geological Survey of the Rocky Mountain Region, 44.) Washington, 1890–91. 2 vols.

GOETHE, J. W. VON. *Faust, Part One.* Translated by Philip Wayne. Harmondsworth, 1949.

GONZALES, LOYS (Ludovicus Gonsalvus). *The Testament of Ignatius Loyola, being Sundry Acts of our Father Ignatius, . . . taken down from the Saint's own lips by Luis Gonzales.* Translated by E. M. Rix. London, 1900.

GROT, NICOLAS VON. "Die Begriffe der Seele und der psychischen Energie in der Psychologie," *Archiv für systematische Philosophie* (Berlin), IV (1898), 257–335.

HARTMANN, CARL ROBERT EDUARD VON. *Philosophie des Unbewussten.* Leipzig, 1869. For translation, see: *Philosophy of the Unconscious.* (English and Foreign Philosophical Library, vols. 25–27.) Translated by W. C. Coupland. London, 1884. 3 vols.

———. *Die Weltanschauung der modernen Physik.* Leipzig, 1909.

HETHERWICK, ALEXANDER. "Some Animistic Beliefs among the Yaos of Central Africa," *Journal of the Royal Anthropological Institute* (London), XXXII (1902), 89–95.

HIPPOLYTUS. *Elenchos.* In: *Hippolytus' Werke,* Vol. III. Edited by Paul Wendland. (Griechische Christliche Schriftsteller.) Leipzig, 1916. For translation, see: *Philosophumena: or, The Refutation of All Heresies.* Translated by Francis Legge. (Translations of Christian Literature.) London and New York, 1921. 2 vols.

[HORAPOLLO NILIACUS.] *The Hieroglyphics of Horapollo.* Translated and edited by George Boas. (Bollingen Series XXIII.) New York, 1950.

HUBERT, HENRI, and MAUSS, MARCEL. *Mélanges d'histoire des religions.* (Travaux de l'Année sociologique.) Paris, 1909.

149

I Ching. The German translation by Richard Wilhelm, rendered into English by Cary F. Baynes. Princeton (Bollingen Series XIX) and London, 3rd edn., 1967.

IGNATIUS OF ANTIOCH, SAINT. *Epistle to the Ephesians.* In: *The Apostolic Fathers.* Translated by Kirsopp Lake. (Loeb Classical Library.) London and New York, 1914. 2 vols. (Vol. I, pp. 173–97.)

IRENAEUS, SAINT. *Contra* [or *Adversus*] *haereses libri quinque.* See MIGNE, *P.G.,* vol. 7, cols. 433–1224. For translation, see: *The Writings of Irenaeus.* Translated by Alexander Roberts and W. H. Rambaut. Vol. I. (Ante-Nicene Christian Library, 5.) Edinburgh, 1868.

JAMES, WILLIAM. "Frederic Myers' Service to Psychology," *Proceedings of the Society for Psychical Research* (London), XVII (1901; pub. 1903), 13–23.

——. *Principles of Psychology.* New York, 1890. 2 vols.

——. *The Varieties of Religious Experience.* London, 1902.

JANET, PIERRE. *L'Automatisme psychologique.* Paris, 1889.

——. *Les Névroses.* Paris. 1909.

JEANS, JAMES. *Physics and Philosophy.* Cambridge, 1942.

JERUSALEM, WILHELM. *Lehrbuch der Psychologie.* 3rd edn., Vienna and Leipzig, 1902.

JORDAN, PASCUAL. "Positivistische Bemerkungen über die parapsychischen Erscheinungen," *Zentralblatt für Psychotherapie* (Leipzig), IX (1936), 3–17.

JUNG, CARL GUSTAV.* "The Aims of Psychotherapy." In: *Collected Works,* vol. 16.

——. *Aion: Researches into the Phenomenology of the Self. Collected Works,* vol. 9, part i.

——. "The Association Method." In: *Experimental Researches. Collected Works,* vol. 2. (Alternative source: *Collected Papers on Analytical Psychology,* q.v.)

——. *Collected Papers on Analytical Psychology.* Edited by Constance Long, translated by various hands. London, 1916; 2nd edn., London, 1917, New York, 1920.

——. "Instinct and the Unconscious." In: *Collected Works,* vol. 8.

* For details of the *Collected Works* of C. G. Jung, see the end of this volume.

——. "Paracelsus as a Spiritual Phenomenon." In: *Collected Works,* vol. 13.

——. "The Phenomenology of the Spirit in Fairytales." In: *Collected Works,* vol. 9, part i.

——. *Psychiatric Studies. Collected Works,* vol. 1.

——. *Psychological Types. Collected Works,* vol. 6. (Alternative source: Translation by H. G. Baynes. London and New York, 1923.)

——. *Psychology and Alchemy. Collected Works,* vol. 12.

——. "The Psychology of Dementia Praecox." In: *Collected Works,* vol. 3.

——. "The Psychology of the Unconscious." In: *Collected Works,* vol. 7.

——. *Studies in Word Association.* In: *Collected Works,* vol. 2. (Alternative source: *Studies in Word-Association* . . . under the direction of C. G. Jung. Translated by M. D. Eder. London, 1918; New York, 1919.)

——. *Symbols of Transformation. Collected Works,* vol. 5.

——. "The Theory of Psychoanalysis." In: *Collected Works,* vol. 4.

——. *Two Essays on Analytical Psychology. Collected Works,* vol. 7.

——. "The Transcendent Function." In: *Collected Works,* vol. 8.

——. *Von den Wurzeln des Bewusstseins.* Zurich, 1954.

——. See also PETERSON; RICKSHER.

KANT, IMMANUEL. *Werke.* Edited by Ernst Cassirer. Berlin, 1912–22. 11 vols. (*Anthropologie,* VIII, pp. 2–228; *Logik,* VIII, pp. 325–452; *Träume eines Geistersehers,* II, pp. 331–90.)

——. *Dreams of a Spirit-Seer, Illustrated by Dreams of Metaphysics.* Translated by Emanuel F. Goerwitz. London, 1900.

KATZ, DAVID. *Animals and Men.* Translated by Hannah Steinberg and Arthur Summerfield. London (Penguin Books), 1953.

KHUNRATH, HEINRICH. *Amphitheatrum sapientiae aeternae solius verae.* Hanau, 1604.

——. *Von hylealischen . . . Chaos.* Magdeburg, 1597.

KOCH-GRÜNBERG, THEODOR. *Südamerikanische Felszeichnungen.* Berlin, 1907.

KÜLPE, OSWALD. *Einleitung in die Philosophie.* 7th edn., Leipzig, 1915.

——. *Outlines of Psychology.* Translated by Edward Bradford Titchener. London and New York, 1895.

LEHMANN, FRIEDRICH RUDOLF. *Mana, der Begriff des "ausserordentlich Wirkungsvollen" bei Südseevölkern.* Leipzig, 1922.

LÉVY-BRUHL, LUCIEN. *How Natives Think.* Translated by Lilian A. Clare. London, 1926. (Orig.: *Les Fonctions mentales dans les sociétés inférieures.* Paris, 1912.)

LEWES, GEORGE HENRY. *Problems of Life and Mind.* London, 1874 [1873]–79. 5 vols. (Vol. II, *The Physical Basis of Mind,* 1877.)

"Liber de compositione Alchemiae." See *Artis auriferae,* **ii.**

LIPPS, THEODOR. "Der Begriff des Unbewussten." In: [*Report of*] *Third International Congress for Psychology,* Munich, 4–7 August 1896. Munich, 1897.

——. *Grundtatsachen des Seelenlebens.* Bonn, 1912.

——. *Leitfaden der Psychologie.* Leipzig, 1903; 2nd edn., 1906.

LOVEJOY, ARTHUR O. "The Fundamental Concept of the Primitive Philosophy," *The Monist* (Chicago), XVI (1906), 357–82.

LUMHOLTZ, CARL. *Unknown Mexico.* London, 1903.

McGEE, W. J. "The Siouan Indians—A Preliminary Sketch." In: *Fifteenth Report of the U.S. Bureau of Ethnology for 1893–94.* Washington, 1897. (Pp. 153–204.)

MAEDER, ALPHONSE. *Heilung und Entwicklung im Seelenleben.* Zurich, 1918.

——. "Régulation psychique et guérison," *Archives suisses de neurologie et de psychiatrie* (Zurich), XVI (1925), 198–224.

MANNHARDT, WILHELM. *Wald- und Feldkulte.* 2nd edn., Berlin, 1904–5. 2 vols.

MARAIS, EUGÈNE NIELEN. *The Soul of the White Ant.* Translated (from the Afrikaans) by Winifred de Kok. London, 1937.

MEIER, CARL ALFRED. "Moderne Physik—Moderne Psychologie." In: *Die kulturelle Bedeutung der komplexen Psychologie.* (Festschrift zum 60. Geburtstag von C. G. Jung.) Berlin, 1935.

MIGNE, JACQUES PAUL (ed.). *Patrologiae cursus completus.*
[*P.L.*] Latin series. Paris, 1844–64. 221 vols.
[*P.G.*] Greek series. Paris, 1857–66. 166 vols.
[These works are cited as "MIGNE, *P.L.*" and "MIGNE, *P.G.*" respectively. References are to columns, not to pages.]

Morgan, Conway Lloyd. *Habit and Instinct.* London, 1896.

Morienus Romanus. See *Theatrum chemicum,* ii.

Myers, Frederic W. H. "The Subliminal Consciousness," *Proceedings of the Society for Psychical Research* (London), VII (1892), 298–355.

Mylius, Johann Daniel. *Philosophia reformata.* Frankfurt, 1622.

Nunberg, H. "On the Physical Accompaniments of Association Processes." In: *Studies in Word-Association* . . . under the direction of C. G. Jung. Translated by M. D. Eder. London, 1918; New York, 1919. (Pp. 531–60.)

Orandus, Eirenaeus. *Nicholas Flammel: His Exposition of the Hieroglyphicall Figures, etc.* London, 1624.

Origen. *In Jeremiam homiliae.* See Migne, *P.G.,* vol. 13, cols. 255–544.

Ostwald, (Friedrich) Wilhelm. *Die Philosophie der Werte.* Leipzig, 1913.

Paracelsus (Theophrastus Bombastes of Hohenheim). *De vita longa.* Edited by Adam von Bodenstein. Basel, 1562.

——. *Sämtliche Werke.* Edited by Karl Sudhoff and Wilhelm Matthiessen. Munich and Berlin, 1922–35. 15 vols.

——. *Erster [–Zehender] Theil der Bücher und Schrifften . . . Philippi Theophrasti Bombast von Hohenheim, Paracelsi genannt.* Edited by Johannes Huser. Basel, 1589–91. 10 vols.

Paulus, Jean. *Le Problème de l'hallucination et l'évolution de la psychologie d'Esquirol à Pierre Janet.* (Bibliothèque de la Faculté de Philosophie et de Lettres de l'Université de Liège, fasc. 91.) Liège and Paris, 1941.

Pechuël-Loesche, Eduard. *Volkskunde von Loango.* Stuttgart, 1907.

Peterson, Frederick, and Jung, C. G. "Psycho-physical Investigations with the Galvanometer and Pneumograph in Normal and Insane Individuals," *Brain* (London), XXX (1907), 153–218.

Picavet, François. *Essais sur l'histoire générale et comparée des théologies et des philosophies médiévales.* Paris, 1913.

Pitra, Jean Baptiste. *Analecta sacra et classica Spicilegio Solesmensi parata.* Paris and Rome, 1876–91. 8 vols.

Preuss, K. T. "Der Ursprung der Religion und Kunst," *Globus* (Brunswick), LXXXVI (1904), 321–92 passim; LXXXVII (1905), 333–419 passim.

Ricksher, C., and Jung, C. G. "Further Investigations on the Galvanic Phenomenon," *Journal of Abnormal and Social Psychology* (Albany, N. Y.), II (1907), 189–217.

Ripley, Sir George. *Opera omnia chemica.* Cassel, 1649.

Rivers, W. H. R. "Instinct and the Unconscious," *British Journal of Psychology* (Cambridge), X (1919–20), 1–7.

Röhr, J. "Das Wesen des Mana," *Anthropos* (Salzburg), XIV–XV (1919–20), 97–124.

Rosencreutz, Christian. *Chymische Hochzeit.* Strasbourg, 1616.

Saint-Graal. Edited by Eugène Hucher. Le Mans, 1878. 3 vols.

Schiller, Friedrich. *On the Aesthetic Education of Man.* Translated by Reginald Snell. London, 1954.

Schultze, Fritz. *Psychologie der Naturvölker.* Leipzig, 1900; another edn., 1925.

Seligmann, Charles Gabriel. *The Melanesians of British New Guinea.* Cambridge, 1910.

Siebeck, Hermann. *Geschichte der Psychologie.* Gotha, 1880–84. 2 parts.

Silberer, Herbert. *Problems of Mysticism and Its Symbolism.* Translated by Smith Ely Jelliffe. New York, 1917.

Söderblom, Nathan. *Das Werden des Gottesglaubens.* Leipzig, 1926.

Spencer, Baldwin, and Gillen, F. J. *The Northern Tribes of Central Australia.* London, 1904.

Stern, L. William. *Über Psychologie der individuellen Differenzen.* (Schriften der Gesellschaft für psychologische Forschung, 12.) Leipzig, 1900.

Szondi, Lipot. *Experimentelle Triebdiagnostik.* Bonn, 1947–49. 2 vols.

——. *Triebpathologie.* Bern, 1952.

THEATRUM CHEMICUM. Ursel and Strasbourg, 1602–61. 6 vols. (Vols. 1–3, Ursel, 1602; etc.)

Contents quoted in this volume:

VOLUME I

i Dorn: Speculativae philosophiae [pp. 255–310]
ii Dorn: Philosophia meditativa [pp. 450–72]

THORNDIKE, LYNN. *A History of Magic and Experimental Science.* New York, 1929–41. 6 vols.

TYLOR, EDWARD B. *Primitive Culture.* 3rd edn., London, 1891. 2 vols.

VERAGUTH, OTTO. *Das psycho-galvanische Reflexphänomen.* Berlin, 1909.

VILLA, GUIDO. *Einleitung in die Psychologie der Gegenwart.* (Translated from Italian.) Leipzig, 1902.

WARNECKE, J. *Die Religion der Batak.* Leipzig, 1909.

WOLF, CHRISTIAN VON. *Psychologia empirica.* Frankfurt and Leipzig, 1732.

——. *Vernünftige Gedanken von Gott, der Welt, und der Seele des Menschen.* 1719.

WUNDT, WILHELM. *Grundzüge der physiologischen Psychologie.* 5th edn., Leipzig, 1902–3. 3 vols.

——. *Outlines of Psychology.* Translated by Charles Hubbard Judd. Leipzig, 1902.

——. *Völkerpsychologie.* Leipzig, 1911–23. 10 vols.

INDEX

A

abstraction, 5

actions: symptomatic, 13, 34; volitional, 82

adaptation, 23, 34*ff;* and direction, 35; harmonious, 39; psychological, libido and, 32; stages towards achievement, 32

Adler, Alfred, 10*n*, 24, 50

affect(s): displacement of, 10; dulling of, 26; estimate of intensity of, 13*f;* in unconscious, 82; value-estimation of, 14

agriculture: libido and, 43; origin of, 43

Agrippa von Nettesheim, Henricus Cornelius, 105

alchemy, 46*f*, 100*ff*

"all-or-none reaction," 91, 97

amplification, of archetypes, 115

anima catholica, see scintilla(e)

animal(s): psychic processes in, 99; *sensus naturae* in, 106

Anthropos, *see* Purusha

antinomian postulate, 23

apperception, in unconscious, 82

apprehension, total, 78

Aratus, 107

arcane substance/arcanum, 100*ff*

archetype(s), 75*f*, 100*ff;* as dynamism, 121; feeling-value of, 119; not an "inborn idea," 136; and instinct, 116; instinctual and archetypal, 121, 128, 129*n;* nature of, 123; numinous character of, 115*f*, 119; as organizers, 141; preconscious, 110, 120; not certainly/exclusively/merely psychic, 125, 140; and religion, 131; scintillae and, 101*f;* as spirit, 115*f*, 126; spontaneous amplification of, 115; *see also* synchronicity

Aristotle, 30

Artis auriferae, 100*n*, 106*n*

assimilation: of unconscious contents, 134

association experiments, 83

astrology, 105, 115*n*

atom-bomb, 128, 130*f*, 132

attitude(s), and progression of libido, 32

Aurora consurgens, 100

automatism(s), 13, 96, 97

B

Bastian, Adolf, 75

behaviour: causality and, 22; pattern(s) of, 111, 115; —, inborn, 75

Berger, Hans, 14*n*

Bergson, Henri, 30

Bible, *see names of individual books*

Binswanger, Ludwig, 14*n*

biology, energic standpoint and, 16

Bleuler, Eugen, 86*f*, 98*n*

Boltzmann, Ludwig, 26

brain psychology, 8, 16

Busemann, Adolf, 87*n*

Busse, Ludwig, 7 & *n*, 17, 18

Butler, Samuel (1612–80), 34*n*

C

Carnot's law, 25

Carpenter, W. B., 89*n*

Carus, C. G., 77, 79, 80, 81

causality: and behaviour, 22; and finality, 4*ff*, 22*ff, see also* finality; and objectivity, 5; psychiatry and, 27; has become relative, 128

cause(s): mechanical and final, 4n; mechanistic/energic views and, 4
cave, Plato's, 123n
censor, 34
centring process, and mythological motifs, 113
ceremonies, for canalizing libido, 44f
Chamberlain, Houston Stewart, 37n
child(ren): brain of, 53; tension of opposites in, 52f; see also dreams; psychology, child-
Christ, coming of, 102
Christianity: substitute formations in, 20; and symbol-formation, 49
Church, as mother, 131
Codrington, Robert Henry, 63, 64n
colour symbolism, 97, 121
complementarity, 139–40n, 142
complex(es), 11ff; in conscious and unconscious, 96f; feeling-toned, in unconscious, 96; nuclear element in, 11f; unconscious, 11n
complex-indicators, 34
complexio oppositorum, 113; God as, 117
conscious: and unconscious, complementarity, 98; see also unconscious
consciousness: approximative, 99; collective, 116, 128f; double, 74, 83, 109; essential to man, 120; field of, 95n; individual differentiation of, 70f; and light, 109; phenomena of, 7; psyche identical with, 94; relation to psyche, 81, 110; relativity of, 110; secondary, 84; semiotic contents, 85; and sense-functions, 85f; subliminal, 77n, 95n; symptomatic contents, 85; unconscious as fringe of, 95
constancy, principle of, 18
Coomaraswamy, Ananda, 108n
Crawley, Ernest, 48n
creative products, in unconscious, 11n
culture: individual, 60; human and "natural," 42; see also work

D

dance/dancing, 42f; buffalo-, 44
dark night of the soul, 135
Darwin, Charles, 23
day-dreaming, see fantasy(-ies)
degeneration, and "getting stuck," 37
Descartes, René, 8n
Dessoir, Max, 77
destruction, mass, 132
development, final, 22, 23; and progression, 37
dissociation(s), 33, 92; of psyche, 83ff; schizophrenic, 96, 97n
dominants, 114, 128; see also archetypes
Dorn, Gerhard, 102f
dragon(s), 36f; hero's fight with, 122
dream(s): children's, 52; Freud and, 89; images in, 100; light-motif in, 109; lumen naturae and, 105; primitives and, 49n
Driesch, Hans, 86, 93
drive(s), 28; energy as, 29; Freud's use of term, 29

E

earth: black, 109; transference of libido to, 43; watery, 101
education, of the adult, 61
effect, cause and, 3f, 31
ego: conscious, and psychic contents, 96f; fragmentation of, 134; not easily altered, 134; second, 96; and self, 134ff; and unconscious, relation, 75
ego-centredness, 136
ego-consciousness, 88, 99, 127; effects of wholeness on, 133; and secondary consciousness, 84, 99
ego-personality, transformation of, 134
Eisler, Robert, 107, 108n

electricity, *see* science, magic and elements, transformation/transmutation of, 47

elixir, 102; *see also* arcane substance

empathy, 5, 32

Empedocles, 30

enantiodromia, 129

energic: and mechanistic standpoints, 3*ff*; —, and psychic events, 6*ff*

energy(-ies): concept of, 4; —, pure and applied, 28; conservation of, 18*ff*; of constellating power in complexes, 12; degree of, and threshold, 82; kinetic, formula for, 143; and physical events, 4, 8; primitive concept of, 64*f*; psychic, *see below;* and quantity, 8*f*; and relation, 6*n*; sexual, 29; specific, of archetypes, 129*n*; —, differentiation of, 15; and substance, 22, 28; transformation of, 41; *see also* force; *mana*

energy, psychic: actual and potential, differentiation, 15; differentiation of libido as, 17; Freud's use of term, 29; history of term, 14*f*; and physical processes, 7; quantitative estimation, 9; varying forms of, 29; *see also* unconscious processes

entropy, 4, 25*ff*, 91; psychological, 26

epiphenomenalism, 7*f*

epistemology/epistemological criticism, 79, 80

equivalence: principle of, 18, 39; in Freud, 19; —, and psychic substitutes, 21

ethics, and sex, conflict, 57

evolution, and progression, 37

extensity, in energy theory, 20

extraversion, and progression, 40

eye(s): as light-symbol, 109; serpent's, 108; seven, 107

Ezekiel, vision of, 108

F

fantasy(-ies): active/creative, 112*ff*; origin of mythical, 38; visual, images in, 100

Faust, see Goethe

Fechner, Gustav Theodor, 74, 76, 82*n*, 129

feeling: and adaptation, 34; directed, 27; function, and values, 10, 144; in unconscious, 82

feeling-tone, complexes and, 11

finality, 5*f*, 23*f*

first half of life, 60

Flamel, Nicholas, 107

Fletcher, Alice, 63

Flournoy, Théodore, 89*n*

force: and energy, confusion, 29; psychic, 15, 31

Franz, Marie-Louise von, 101*n*

Freud, Sigmund, 10*n*, 13, 24, 49, 51, 55*f*, 89*f*, 110; and "censor," 34; on instinct and unconscious, 110*n*; and libido, 29; and pleasure, 50; and sexuality, 19, 22, 29, 51, 55*f*; theory of repression, 11*n*; *see also* psychoanalysis

Frobenius, Leo, 36

function(s): and adaptation, 34; apportionment of libido among, 47; biological adaptive, 86; and compensation, 35*f*; and the psychic, 91

Funk, Philippe, 108*n*

G

Gatschet, Albert Samuel, 49

Germany, 80, 135

Gillen, F. J., 44*n*, 48*n*, 62*n*, 63*n*

glands, instincts and, 90

Gnosticism, 54, 100*n*

God: bacchantic, 80; contradictoriness of, 55; idea of, and *mana*, 65; and imperfect creation, 54; as spirit/spirit of, 54, 80, 100; and Sun, Elgonyi view, 119

gods, as libido analogues, 48*f*
Goethe, J. W. von, 37, 60, 97*n*, 122
Gonzales, Loys, 108
Gottesminne, 20
Grot, Nicolas von, 7, 8, 15
Guillaume de Conches, 106
Gulielmus Parisiensis/Alvernus, *see* Guillaume de Conches; William of Auvergne

H

Hartmann, Eduard von, 3*n*, 6*n*, 20*n*, 77, 88
heaven, as light-symbol, 109
Hegel, G. W. F., 79, 80
Heraclitus, 53
Herbart, J. F., 73
hero-myth, *see* dragon
Hetherwick, Alexander, 62
hexagram, *see* I Ching
Hippolytus, 107, 108*f*
Hiroshima, 128
Holy Ghost, 104; world-soul and, 106
Horapollo, 105*n*, 108
hormones, *see* glands
Hubert, Henri, 28*n*
Hudibras, see Butler, Samuel
hypnotism, 142

I

I Ching, 115*n*
idea(s): archetypal, *see* images, archetypal; elementary, 75; inborn, 75, 136; Platonic, 101; universal, 128
Idealism, German, 79
identification(s): in Hegel, 80; of subjective with collective consciousness, 131
Ignatius (of Antioch), St., 108
Ignatius Loyola, St., 108

image(s): in active fantasy, 112*ff;* archetypal, 123; represents meaning of instinct, 111; symbolical, 100
imagination: active, 114, 121; in unconscious, 82
impulses, natural, 128
incest, and civilization, 23
indeterminism, 91*n*
Indian(s): Mexican, 63; North American, 44, 61*f*, 63; —, South American, 46
individuation, 40, 51, 112, 135*f;* change involved in, 133; religion and, 59
inflation: ego/subjective, 131; in Hegel, 80; social/national, 131
inhibition: of unconscious/and unconsciousness, 34
instinct(s), 90*ff, et passim;* compulsiveness, 92; curbing of, 54; Freudian theory and, 55; Freud's use of term, 29; imitation of, 42; no amorphous, 111; physiological and psychological, 90; repression of, 20; two aspects of, 122
integration: pathological attempts at, 134; of unconscious contents into consciousness, 133
introversion, as regression, 40
intuition, retrospective, 52
involution, 37
Irenaeus, 101*n*
"isms," 85, 116, 129, 131, 132

J

James, William, 77*n*, 84*n*, 95 & *n*, 121
Janet, Pierre, 21, 74, 89, 90, 91*n*, 96
Jeans, Sir James, 123*n*, 144
Jerusalem, W., 90*n*
John, Gospel of, 102*n*, 109, 130
John of the Cross, St., 135
Jordan, Pascual, 141*n*
judgment, in unconscious, 82

Jung, Carl Gustav:
WORKS: "The Aims of Psychotherapy," 112*n; Aion,* 109*n;* "The Association Method," 14*n;* "Instinct and the Unconscious," 10*n;* "Paracelsus as a Spiritual Phenomenon," 105*n;* "The Phenomenology of the Spirit in Fairytales," 126, 132; *Psychiatric Studies,* 11*n; Psychological Types,* 23*n,* 28*n,* 41, 55*n,* 61, 109*n,* 118; *Psychology and Alchemy,* 100*n,* 106*n,* 114*n,* 119*n;* "The Psychology of Dementia Praecox," 10*n,* 12, 13*n; Studies in Word Association,* 10*n,* 14*n; Symbols of Transformation,* 3*n,* 18, 21*n,* 24, 30*n,* 36, 41, 42*n,* 43*n,* 48*n,* 55*n;* "The Theory of Psychoanalysis," 30; *Two Essays on Analytical Psychology,* 28*n,* 65*n,* 112*n,* 114*n,* 119*n; see also* Peterson; Ricksher

damming up of, 38, 58; disappearance of, and equivalence, 19*f;* excess, 47*f,* 49; Freud's synonyms for, 29; justification of term, 29*f;* life-energy as, 17; metaphysical aspect, 30; primitive conception, 61*ff;* progression and regression of, 32*ff;* sexuality and, 30; similarities and differences, 21; stoppage of, 32*f;* symbols as analogues, 48; *see also* adaptation
life, first/second half of, 60
light: wave-lengths, 85; wave and particle theories, 94, 139; see also *lumen*
limbo, psychic, 90
Lipps, Theodor, 15, 16, 76, 82*f,* 124
Lovejoy, Arthur O., 61*n,* 62*n,* 64
lumen, 101; *naturae,* 102
Lumholtz, Carl, 63
luminosity(-ies), 99*ff; see also* self, "uniting" symbols of

K

Kant, Immanuel, 34*n,* 75, 79
Katz, David, 83*n*
Khunrath, Heinrich, 100*ff,* 109
knowledge, psychic system and, 81; *see also* epistemology
Koch-Grünberg, Theodor, 46*n*
Külpe, Oswald, 7 & *n,* 90*n*

L

Lasswitz, 7
Lehmann, Alfred, 14*n*
Lehmann, Friedrich Rudolf, 28*n,* 65
Lévy-Bruhl, Lucien, 44*n,* 49*n,* 50*n,* 63*n,* 65
Lewes, George Henry, 82*n,* 89*n*
libido, 143; apportionment among functions, 47; bases of concept, 3*ff,* 30*f;* canalization of, 41*ff,* 47;

M

McGee, W. J., 61*n*
machine, life and use of, 42
Maeder, Alphonse, 10*n,* 15*n*
magic, 46, 61*ff;* "mother of science," 46; *see also* ceremonies
man: First, 109; inner, 104; responsible, 118; *see also* mass men; medieval man
mana, 28*n,* 63*f,* 65, 119, 143
mandala, 123, 137*f; see also* self, "uniting" symbols of
Mannhardt, Wilhelm, 43*n,* 44*n*
Marais, E. N., 90*n*
mass man, 118, 129, 130
matter: latent psyche in, 144; and psyche, relation, 125, 144; and spirit, 126
maturity, need of education in, 60
Mauss, Marcel, 28*n*
Mayer, Robert, 65*n*

measurement: in psychology, 6*ff;* and values, 9

mechanistic and energic standpoints, 3*ff*

medieval man, 129*f,* 131

megalomania, of schizophrenia, 80

Meier, C. A., 98*n,* 142

memory: slips of, 13; in unconscious, 82

Mercurius, 101*n,* 106

Meringer, R., 43

"micropsychic," 87*n*

mind: as spark, 101; "spirit" and "ghost," 54; as sum of ancestral minds, 54

Monad(s), 102, 109

Monoimos, 108*f*

morality, and sex, 56*f*

Morienus Romanus, 100*n,* 106

movement, and energy, 5

multiplicity, in fantasy, 113

Myers, F. W. H., 77*n,* 80*n,* 95*n*

Mylius, Johann Daniel, 100*n*

mysticism, 135

myth(s): as explanations, 37*f; see also* dragon; hero-myth; night sea journey

mythologems, 105, 137

mythology, 113

N

"natural" and "spiritual," 52

neurosis(-es), 89; dissociation and, 33; psychology of, 96; treatment of, and equivalence principle, 19

Nicholas of Cusa, 117

Nicholas of Flüe, vision of, 121

Nietzsche, F. W., 58, 70, 80, 111

night sea journey, 36*f*

numen, 101, 143

numinosity, 96, 101; of archetypes, 115

Nunberg, H., 14*n*

O

observer, in physics, *see* physics

old, the, and libido in dance, 44

opposites: and libido, 32*f;* —, in child, 52*f;* in God, 55; and progress of culture, 59; union of, 113, 117; see also *complexio oppositorum:* INSTANCES: light/dark, 113; nature/spirit, 51; physical/spiritual passion, 122; right/left, 113; spirit/instinct, 117*f;* upper/lower, 113

Orandus, Eirenaeus, 107*n*

order, in fantasy, 113

organic systems, production of, 91

organological standpoint, 87

Origen, 132*n*

Ostwald, (Friedrich) Wilhelm, 6*n,* 12*n*

P

pan-psychism, 16

Paracelsus, 101, 102, 103*ff*

parallelism, psychophysical, *see* psyche, and the physical, relation

parents: substitute, fantasies of, 20; *see also* father

"parties supérieures / inférieures," 21, 90*ff*

passion, physical and spiritual, 122

Paul, St., conversion of, 121

Pauli, W., 139*n,* 142

Paulus, Jean, 89*n*

Pechuël-Loesche, Eduard, 43*n,* 62*n*

perception, in unconscious, 82

personality, double, 96; *see also* consciousness, double

personification, 66

Peterson, Frederick, and Jung, C. G., 14*n*

philosophy: Eastern, introspective character of, 138; German, powerwords in, 80*f;* Indian, and super-consciousness, 88*n*

physics: atomic, and psyche, 144; and models, 124*f; * observer in, 125, 139*f* & *n;* and psychology, 126*f,* 142
Picavet, François, 106*n*
Pitra, Jean-Baptiste, 107*n*
Plato, 30; cave myth, 123*n*
pleasure, *see* Freud
polytheism, extermination of, 49
"powers," suprapersonal, subjection to, *see* primitives, psychology of
prestige, psychology of, 50
Preuss, K. T., 42*n,* 65
primitives: and canalization of libido, 44*f;* conceptions of libido, 61*ff;* and dreams, 49*n;* and magic, 46; and myths, 38; psychology of, 50; quasi-neurosis of, 50; symbol and, 25; and synchronicity, 50; *see also* magic
probability, 138*f*
process(es): and instincts, 90; psychic, 76, 117
progression: and development, 37; energic view, 38*f;* and extraversion, 40; of libido, 32*ff;* means to regression, 40; origin of, 39
projection(s), 117; in child, on to parents, 53
Protestantism, 59
psyche: conflict between instinct and will, 93; a conscious-unconscious whole, 110; dissociability of, 83*ff;* energic aspects of, 143; whether identical with consciousness, 94, 97, 110; infantile, 51; mass, 131, 132; and matter, relation, 125; as object of experience, 6; and the physical, relation, 7, 17*f;* primitive, 50; relation to consciousness, 81; as relatively closed system, 7, 8, 26; upper and lower limits, 92*f;* the world's pivot, 127 *et passim*
psychiatry, and causality, 27
psychic: how defined, 91; energy of the, 22, 31; *see also* energy, psy-

chic; its nature unconscious, 124; one-sidedness, 117
psychoanalysis, 27, 34*f,* 49; *see also* Freud
psycho-galvanic phenomena, 14
"psychoid," 86*f,* 93*f*
psychology: child-, 52; —, first use of term, 71; has no outside base, 133; position in universities, 72; *see also* brain psychology; consciousness; physics
psychopathology, 134*f*
psychosomatic phenomena, 142
pulse curve, 14
Purusha, 108, 109

Q

quantities(-y): factor of energy, 20; measurement of, and energy, 8*f,* 15; psychic, 15
quintessence, 102*n*

R

rapture, *see* numinosity
reaction(s), *see* "all-or-none" reaction
reason, relativity of, 25
reciprocal action, body-psyche, *see* psyche, and the physical, relation
reduction, 50, 58
reflection, 33; in unconscious, 82
reflex(es), 86
regression, 23; energic view of, 38*f;* and introversion, 40; of libido, 32*ff;* origin of, 39
religion(s): and archetypes, 131; collective, inadequacy of, 59; and collective consciousness, 131; individual, 58*f;* problem of, 51; psychology of, and archetypes, 115; state, 49
representations, 75, 76, 82; Herbart on, 73; primitive, 65

repression(s), 10; of contents of collective unconscious, 129; Freud and, 11*n*, 19, 55, 89
respiration curve, 14
Revelation, Book of, 130*n*
Rhine, J. B., 143
Ricksher, C., 14*n*
Rig-Veda, 108
Ripley, Sir George, 106
rites d'entrée, see ceremonies
Rivers, W. H. R., 91
rock-drawings, South American, *see* magic
Röhr, J., 65
Rosencreutz, Christian, 47*n*
rotation, 113

S

Schelling, F. W. J. von, 75, 79
Schiller, Friedrich, 14
schizophrenia, blunting of affect in, 26
schizophrenics, megalomania of, 80
Schopenhauer, Arthur, 30, 79, 80, 81
Schultze, Fritz, 42*n*
science: magic and, 46; one-sidedness of, 130
scintilla(e), 100*ff*, 109
second half of life, 60
self: and ego, 134*ff*; subordination of will to, 134; "uniting" symbols of, 109
Seligmann, Charles Gabriel, 64*n*
sensation, unanalysable, 73
sense-functions, and consciousness, 85
sensus naturae, 105*n*
serpent(s): in vision of St. Ignatius Loyola, 108; and zodiac, 107; *see also* uroboros
sexualism, *see* drive(s)
sexuality: Freud and, 19, 22, 29, 51, 55*f*; importance in psychic life, 57; incomplete explanation of

psychic phenomena, 21*n*; infantile, 51; and libido, 30; as strongest instinct, 58; young people and, 60
"sexual" question, 56
shadow: man without a, 118; realization of the, 118, 131
Siebeck, Hermann, 69*n*
Silberer, Herbert, 47*n*
sin, original, 130
snake(s), *see* serpent; uroboros
Söderblom, Nathan, 54*n*, 64
Sophocles, 108
soul(s): cortical/medullary, 87; dark part of the, 81; multiple/plurality of, 84; psychology and the, 69*f*, 77; *see also* dark night of the soul; psyche; spirit(s)
soul-spark(s), 135; *see also* scintilla(e)
sound-frequencies, 85
space-continuum, relative, 141
sparks, 100*ff; see also* soul-spark
species, development of, 86
spectrum, *see* colour-symbolism
Spencer, B., 44*n*, 48*n*, 62*n*, 63*n*
spirit(s): antithesis with instinct, 117; archetype as, 115*f*, 126; and instinct, as limiting will, 93; meaning of term, 54; and sexuality, 57; sovereignty of, 80; two-faced, 132; *see also* mind; psyche; soul
splitting of personality, 33, 83*f; see also* consciousness
star(s): in man, 103; *see also* self, "uniting" symbols of
State, philosophy of the, 80
statistical laws, 139
Stern, L. W., 15 & *n*
subconscious(ness), 74, 78, 87*f*, 96, 97
subcortical processes, *see* "psychoid"
subject: and psychic processes, 83; unconscious, 75
sublimation(s), 22, 58; forced, 59

"subliminal," 82, 84*f*
substance, and energy, 22; *see also* mechanistic and energic standpoints
substitute formations, 19
superconsciousness, 74, 78, 88
superman, 80
symbol(s): alchemical, 46, 100*f;* cause and, 24*f;* formation of, 45*ff,* 61; in Freudian literature, 85; "libido analogues," 48; semiotic interpretation, 46; "uniting," 109; *see also* dream symbols
"symbola," 59
symbolism: catholic, 59; colour, 97, 121
symptom(s): in neurosis, 34; psychogenic, and unconscious, 89
symptoma/symptosis, 127
synchronicity, 115*n*, 125, 141*ff;* of archetypal events, 108

T

teleology, 4*n*
telepathy, *see* synchronicity
theosophy, 59
thinking: directed, 27; function, and adaptation, 34
Thorndike, Lynn, 106*n*
thought-deprivation, *see* automatism(s)
threshold: lower and upper, 86; psychological, 76*n*, 81*f*, 86
time: in association experiments, 13; symbolism, 107*f; see also* spacetime continuum
touch, magic, *see* dance/dancing
trance, *see* synchronicity
transformation, energic, 41
transmutation of elements, *see* elements
truth, identification with one-sided, *see* consciousness, collective
Tylor, E. B., 62
types, in man, 111

U

unconscious, 33*f, et passim;* compensatory function of, 10; and consciousness, complementarity, 98; contents of, 75, 95; Fechner and Lipps on, 76; Freud's view, 89; fringe of conscious, 95; personal, 110; —, contents of, *see separate entry below;* statements about it unverifiable, 124; subject of, 87; as unknown psychic, 95; Wundt's view, 74
unconscious contents: dreams as mediators of, 89; integration into consciousness, 120*f*, 133; "representedness" of, 75
unconscious processes, and energy, 16
uniformity, psychic, 137
universals, 5*n*
uroboros, 108, 123

V

values: comparison of, 9*ff;* conscious, disappearance of, 10; subjective, 9*f;* unconscious, 10
Veraguth, Otto, 14*n*
Villa, Guido, 74*n*
vitalism, *see* drive(s)
volition: presupposes choosing subject, 93; *see also* will

W

war, *see* atom-bomb
Warnecke, J., 64*n*
wholeness: conscious, 135*n;* preconscious, 135; psychic, 85; unconscious, 121
will, 91*ff;* biological motivation of, 93; and function, 92; and instinct, 110; primitives and, 45; in Schopenhauer, 80; subordina-

will (*cont.*)
    tion to self, 134; in unconscious,
    82; unconscious acts of, 83, 84
William of Auvergne, 106
Wisdom of Solomon, 101
Wolf, Christian von, 71, 75
work: culture and, 41; energy and,
    41*f*
world-soul, *see* scintilla

Wundt, Wilhelm, 3*n*, 4*n*, 6 & *n*, 16,
    22, 23, 74*ff*, 82, 83

Z

Zacharias, Book of, 107*n*
Zen Buddhism, 135
Zorobabel, 107

THE COLLECTED WORKS OF
C. G. JUNG

T HE PUBLICATION of the first complete edition, in English, of the works of C. G. Jung was undertaken by Routledge and Kegan Paul, Ltd., in England and by Bollingen Foundation in the United States. The American edition is number XX in Bollingen Series, which since 1967 has been published by Princeton University Press. The edition contains revised versions of works previously published, such as *Psychology of the Unconscious*, which is now entitled *Symbols of Transformation*; works originally written in English, such as *Psychology and Religion*; works not previously translated, such as *Aion*; and, in general, new translations of virtually all of Professor Jung's writings. Prior to his death, in 1961, the author supervised the textual revision, which in some cases is extensive. Sir Herbert Read (d. 1968), Dr. Michael Fordham, and Dr. Gerhard Adler compose the Editorial Committee; the translator is R. F. C. Hull (except for Volume 2) and William McGuire is executive editor.

The price of the volumes varies according to size; they are sold separately, and may also be obtained on standing order. Several of the volumes are extensively illustrated. Each volume contains an index and in most a bibliography; the final volume will contain a complete bibliography of Professor Jung's writings and a general index to the entire edition.

In the following list, dates of original publication are given in parentheses (of original composition, in brackets). Multiple dates indicate revisions.

*1. PSYCHIATRIC STUDIES

On the Psychology and Pathology of So-Called Occult Phenomena
(1902)

On Hysterical Misreading (1904)

Cryptomnesia (1905)

On Manic Mood Disorder (1903)

A Case of Hysterical Stupor in a Prisoner in Detention (1902)

On Simulated Insanity (1903)

A Medical Opinion on a Case of Simulated Insanity (1904)

A Third and Final Opinion on Two Contradictory Psychiatric Diagnoses (1906)

On the Psychological Diagnosis of Facts (1905)

2. EXPERIMENTAL RESEARCHES

Translated by Leopold Stein in collaboration with Diana Riviere

STUDIES IN WORD ASSOCIATION (1904–7, 1910)

The Associations of Normal Subjects (by Jung and F. Riklin)

An Analysis of the Associations of an Epileptic

The Reaction-Time Ratio in the Association Experiment

Experimental Observations on the Faculty of Memory

Psychoanalysis and Association Experiments

The Psychological Diagnosis of Evidence

Association, Dream, and Hysterical Symptom

The Psychopathological Significance of the Association Experiment

Disturbances in Reproduction in the Association Experiment

The Association Method

The Family Constellation

PSYCHOPHYSICAL RESEARCHES (1907–8)

On the Psychophysical Relations of the Association Experiment

Psychophysical Investigations with the Galvanometer and Pneumograph in Normal and Insane Individuals (by F. Peterson and Jung)

Further Investigations on the Galvanic Phenomenon and Respiration in Normal and Insane Individuals (by C. Ricksher and Jung)

Appendix: Statistical Details of Enlistment (1906); New Aspects of Criminal Psychology (1908); The Psychological Methods of Investigation Used in the Psychiatric Clinic of the University of Zurich (1910); On the Doctrine of Complexes ([1911] 1913); On the Psychological Diagnosis of Evidence (1937)

* Published 1957; 2nd edn., 1970.

*3. THE PSYCHOGENESIS OF MENTAL DISEASE
     The Psychology of Dementia Praecox (1907)
     The Content of the Psychoses (1908/1914)
     On Psychological Understanding (1914)
     A Criticism of Bleuler's Theory of Schizophrenic Negativism (1911)
     On the Importance of the Unconscious in Psychopathology (1914)
     On the Problem of Psychogenesis in Mental Disease (1919)
     Mental Disease and the Psyche (1928)
     On the Psychogenesis of Schizophrenia (1939)
     Recent Thoughts on Schizophrenia (1957)
     Schizophrenia (1958)

†4. FREUD AND PSYCHOANALYSIS
     Freud's Theory of Hysteria: A Reply to Aschaffenburg (1906)
     The Freudian Theory of Hysteria (1908)
     The Analysis of Dreams (1909)
     A Contribution to the Psychology of Rumour (1910–11)
     On the Significance of Number Dreams (1910–11)
     Morton Prince, "The Mechanism and Interpretation of Dreams": A
          Critical Review (1911)
     On the Criticism of Psychoanalysis (1910)
     Concerning Psychoanalysis (1912)
     The Theory of Psychoanalysis (1913)
     General Aspects of Psychoanalysis (1913)
     Psychoanalysis and Neurosis (1916)
     Some Crucial Points in Psychoanalysis: A Correspondence between
          Dr. Jung and Dr. Loÿ (1914)
     Prefaces to "Collected Papers on Analytical Psychology" (1916, 1917)
     The Significance of the Father in the Destiny of the Individual
          (1909/1949)
     Introduction to Kranefeldt's "Secret Ways of the Mind" (1930)
     Freud and Jung: Contrasts (1929)

‡5. SYMBOLS OF TRANSFORMATION (1911–12/1952)
          PART I
     Introduction
     Two Kinds of Thinking
     The Miller Fantasies: Anamnesis
     The Hymn of Creation
     The Song of the Moth   (continued)

* Published 1960.   † Published 1961.
‡ Published 1956; 2nd edn., 1967. (65 plates, 43 text figures.)

5. *(continued)*
    PART II
    Introduction
    The Concept of Libido
    The Transformation of Libido
    The Origin of the Hero
    Symbols of the Mother and of Rebirth
    The Battle for Deliverance from the Mother
    The Dual Mother
    The Sacrifice
    Epilogue
    Appendix: The Miller Fantasies

*6. PSYCHOLOGICAL TYPES (1921)
    Introduction
    The Problem of Types in the History of Classical and Medieval
        Thought
    Schiller's Ideas on the Type Problem
    The Apollinian and the Dionysian
    The Type Problem in Human Character
    The Type Problem in Poetry
    The Type Problem in Psychopathology
    The Type Problem in Aesthetics
    The Type Problem in Modern Philosophy
    The Type Problem in Biography
    General Description of the Types
    Definitions
    Epilogue
    Four Papers on Psychological Typology (1913, 1925, 1931, 1936)

†7. TWO ESSAYS ON ANALYTICAL PSYCHOLOGY
    On the Psychology of the Unconscious (1917/1926/1943)
    The Relations between the Ego and the Unconscious (1928)
    Appendix: New Paths in Psychology (1912); The Structure of the
        Unconscious (1916) (new versions, with variants, 1966)

‡8. THE STRUCTURE AND DYNAMICS OF THE PSYCHE
    On Psychic Energy (1928)
    The Transcendent Function ([1916]/1957)
    A Review of the Complex Theory (1934)
    The Significance of Constitution and Heredity in Psychology (1929)

---

* Published 1971.   † Published 1953; 2nd edn., 1966.
‡ Published 1960; 2nd edn., 1969.

Psychological Factors Determining Human Behavior (1937)
Instinct and the Unconscious (1919)
The Structure of the Psyche (1927/1931)
On the Nature of the Psyche (1947/1954)
General Aspects of Dream Psychology (1916/1948)
On the Nature of Dreams (1945/1948)
The Psychological Foundations of Belief in Spirits (1920/1948)
Spirit and Life (1926)
Basic Postulates of Analytical Psychology (1931)
Analytical Psychology and *Weltanschauung* (1928/1931)
The Real and the Surreal (1933)
The Stages of Life (1930–1931)
The Soul and Death (1934)
Synchronicity: An Acausal Connecting Principle (1952)
Appendix: On Synchronicity (1951)

*9. PART I. THE ARCHETYPES AND THE
      COLLECTIVE UNCONSCIOUS
Archetypes of the Collective Unconscious (1934/1954)
The Concept of the Collective Unconscious (1936)
Concerning the Archetypes, with Special Reference to the Anima
      Concept (1936/1954)
Psychological Aspects of the Mother Archetype (1938/1954)
Concerning Rebirth (1940/1950)
The Psychology of the Child Archetype (1940)
The Psychological Aspects of the Kore (1941)
The Phenomenology of the Spirit in Fairytales (1945/1948)
On the Psychology of the Trickster-Figure (1954)
Conscious, Unconscious, and Individuation (1939)
A Study in the Process of Individuation (1934/1950)
Concerning Mandala Symbolism (1950)
Appendix: Mandalas (1955)

*9. PART II. AION (1951)
      RESEARCHES INTO THE PHENOMENOLOGY OF THE SELF
The Ego
The Shadow
The Syzygy: Anima and Animus
The Self
Christ, a Symbol of the Self
The Sign of the Fishes   (*continued*)

* Published 1959; 2nd edn., 1968. (Part I: 79 plates, with 29 in colour.)

9. (*continued*)
   The Prophecies of Nostradamus
   The Historical Significance of the Fish
   The Ambivalence of the Fish Symbol
   The Fish in Alchemy
   The Alchemical Interpretation of the Fish
   Background to the Psychology of Christian Alchemical Symbolism
   Gnostic Symbols of the Self
   The Structure and Dynamics of the Self
   Conclusion

*10. CIVILIZATION IN TRANSITION
   The Role of the Unconscious (1918)
   Mind and Earth (1927/1931)
   Archaic Man (1931)
   The Spiritual Problem of Modern Man (1928/1931)
   The Love Problem of a Student (1928)
   Woman in Europe (1927)
   The Meaning of Psychology for Modern Man (1933/1934)
   The State of Psychotherapy Today (1934)
   Preface and Epilogue to "Essays on Contemporary Events" (1946)
   Wotan (1936)
   After the Catastrophe (1945)
   The Fight with the Shadow (1946)
   The Undiscovered Self (Present and Future) (1957)
   Flying Saucers: A Modern Myth (1958)
   A Psychological View of Conscience (1958)
   Good and Evil in Analytical Psychology (1959)
   Introduction to Wolff's "Studies in Jungian Psychology" (1959)
   The Swiss Line in the European Spectrum (1928)
   Reviews of Keyserling's "America Set Free" (1930) and "La Révolution Mondiale" (1934)
   The Complications of American Psychology (1930)
   The Dreamlike World of India (1939)
   What India Can Teach Us (1939)
   Appendix: Documents (1933–1938)

†11. PSYCHOLOGY AND RELIGION: WEST AND EAST
   WESTERN RELIGION
   Psychology and Religion (The Terry Lectures) (1938/1940)

* Published 1964; 2nd edn., 1970. (8 plates.)
† Published 1958; 2nd edn., 1969.

A Psychological Approach to the Dogma of the Trinity (1942/1948)
Transformation Symbolism in the Mass (1942/1954)
Forewords to White's "God and the Unconscious" and Werblowsky's "Lucifer and Prometheus" (1952)
Brother Klaus (1933)
Psychotherapists or the Clergy (1932)
Psychoanalysis and the Cure of Souls (1928)
Answer to Job (1952)
EASTERN RELIGION
Psychological Commentaries on "The Tibetan Book of the Great Liberation" (1939/1954) and "The Tibetan Book of the Dead" (1935/1953)
Yoga and the West (1936)
Foreword to Suzuki's "Introduction to Zen Buddhism" (1939)
The Psychology of Eastern Meditation (1943)
The Holy Men of India: Introduction to Zimmer's "Der Weg zum Selbst" (1944)
Foreword to the "I Ching" (1950)

*12. PSYCHOLOGY AND ALCHEMY (1944)
Prefatory note to the English Edition ([1951?] added 1967)
Introduction to the Religious and Psychological Problems of Alchemy
Individual Dream Symbolism in Relation to Alchemy (1936)
Religious Ideas in Alchemy (1937)
Epilogue

†13. ALCHEMICAL STUDIES
Commentary on "The Secret of the Golden Flower" (1929)
The Visions of Zosimos (1938/1954)
Paracelsus as a Spiritual Phenomenon (1942)
The Spirit Mercurius (1943/1948)
The Philosophical Tree (1945/1954)

‡14. MYSTERIUM CONIUNCTIONIS (1955-56)
AN INQUIRY INTO THE SEPARATION AND
SYNTHESIS OF PSYCHIC OPPOSITES IN ALCHEMY
The Components of the Coniunctio
The Paradoxa
The Personification of the Opposites
Rex and Regina   (continued)

* Published 1953; 2nd edn., completely revised, 1968. (270 illustrations.)
† Published 1968. (50 plates, 4 text figures.)
‡ Published 1963; 2nd edn., 1970. (10 plates.)

14. (*continued*)
   Adam and Eve
   The Conjunction

*15. THE SPIRIT IN MAN, ART, AND LITERATURE
   Paracelsus (1929)
   Paracelsus the Physician (1941)
   Sigmund Freud in His Historical Setting (1932)
   In Memory of Sigmund Freud (1939)
   Richard Wilhelm: In Memoriam (1930)
   On the Relation of Analytical Psychology to Poetry (1922)
   Psychology and Literature (1930/1950)
   "Ulysses": A Monologue (1932)
   Picasso (1932)

†16. THE PRACTICE OF PSYCHOTHERAPY
   GENERAL PROBLEMS OF PSYCHOTHERAPY
   Principles of Practical Psychotherapy (1935)
   What Is Psychotherapy? (1935)
   Some Aspects of Modern Psychotherapy (1930)
   The Aims of Psychotherapy (1931)
   Problems of Modern Psychotherapy (1929)
   Psychotherapy and a Philosophy of Life (1943)
   Medicine and Psychotherapy (1945)
   Psychotherapy Today (1945)
   Fundamental Questions of Psychotherapy (1951)
   SPECIFIC PROBLEMS OF PSYCHOTHERAPY
   The Therapeutic Value of Abreaction (1921/1928)
   The Practical Use of Dream-Analysis (1934)
   The Psychology of the Transference (1946)
   Appendix: The Realities of Practical Psychotherapy ([1937] added, 1966)

‡17. THE DEVELOPMENT OF PERSONALITY
   Psychic Conflicts in a Child (1910/1946)
   Introduction to Wickes's "Analyses der Kinderseele" (1927/1931)
   Child Development and Education (1928)
   Analytical Psychology and Education: Three Lectures (1926/1946)
   The Gifted Child (1943)
   The Significance of the Unconscious in Individual Education (1928)

* Published 1966.
† Published 1954; 2nd edn., revised and augmented, 1966. (13 illustrations.)
‡ Published 1954.

The Development of Personality (1934)
Marriage as a Psychological Relationship (1925)

18. MISCELLANY
Posthumous and Other Miscellaneous Works

19. BIBLIOGRAPHY AND INDEX
Complete Bibliography of C. G. Jung's Writings
General Index to the Collected Works